CONTENTS

Ships in Focus Publications

Correspondence and editorial:
Roy Fenton
18 Durrington Avenue
London SW20 8NT
020 8879 3527
rfenton@rfenton.demon.co.uk
Orders and photographic:
John & Marion Clarkson
18 Franklands, Longton
Preston PR4 5PD
01772 612855
sales@shipsinfocus.co.uk

Printed by The Amadeus Press,
Cleckheaton, West Yorkshire.
Designed by Hugh Smallwood,
John Clarkson and Roy Fenton.
SHIPS IN FOCUS RECORD
ISBN 1 901703 126

SHIPS IN FOCUS RECORD 15

We are pleased to report that our requests for help with finding specific photographs for future issues of *Record* had a response which exceeded our expectations, and all but one of our needs were met. It is particularly pleasing that a French reader could supply photographs of most of the later PLM ships, very few of which seem to feature in UK collections. Those responding have been acknowledged individually, but a 'thank you' goes out to all readers who wrote. *Help put it on Record* appears on page 163 in this issue: we do hope you will read it and respond if you can.

Our move to quarterly publication inevitably compressed the time frame for receiving letters between *Records* 13 and 14, and hence *Putting the Record straight* was unusually short in *Record* 14. However, letters and photographs have continued to flow in and the column has been extended in this issue to accommodate them.

Continuing the parish notices, Mr Smith of The Bindery has told us that he can no longer bind copies of *Record* (or, indeed, any other journal) as his business is now concentrating on book production. We are seeking an alternative binder, who can offer the same high standard of workmanship, and any suggestions from readers would be welcomed.

Most *Record* readers in the UK who ordered a copy of *British Shipping Fleets* will have received it just in time for Christmas. The finish was something of a cliffhanger, as the delay was in large part due to a problem reproducing scanned photographs. Our printer was dissatisfied with the initial run and decided to scrap it. With quality our major concern as publishers, this was a decision we fully endorsed, accepting the inevitable delay. One or two customers report that their copies were slightly damaged in transit. Despite our taking great care with packing, this may happen from time to time, especially near Christmas. But please, will any reader who receives any damaged publication direct from us let us know, and we will replace it.

Reactions to *British Shipping Fleets* have been positive, and we have already received a number of notes which will appear in a future *Record*. For those still without a copy, details appear opposite.

John Clarkson   Roy Fenton
January 2001

SUBSCRIPTION RATES FOR RECORD

Subscribers make a saving on the postage of three issues, and receive each *Record* just as soon as it is published. They are also eligible for concessions on newly-published *Ships in Focus* titles. Readers can start their subscription with *any* issue, and are welcome to backdate it to receive previous issues.

UK	£23
Europe (airmail)	£25
Rest of world (surface mail)	£25
Rest of world (airmail)	£30

Vandyck (2) at Southampton, 6th May 1933 (see page 144). *[F.W. Hawks]*

Fleet in Focus
FURNESS NORTH PACIFIC SHIPS Part 2
David Burrell

PACIFIC GROVE

Deutsche Werke Kiel AG, Kiel; 1928, 7,114gt, 450 feet

Two oil engines 6-cyl. 4SCSA by Deutsche Werke Kiel AG, Kiel; 5,000 BHP, 13 knots

Pacific Grove earned more decorations than any other Furness ship, eleven. Transferred early to the Atlantic, she was in London's Surrey Commercial Docks when the Dunkirk evacuation commenced, and her lifeboats lifted troops off the French beaches. On the morning of 23rd September 1940, north west of Tory Island, she was attacked by an Fw200 Condor of KG40. A 500lb bomb lodged, unexploded, in the accommodation. Third officer Norman Watson, bosun Lars Jensen and chief cook Samuel McEachran manhandled it over the side. Watson was awarded the George Medal, the others the British Empire Medal. All received Lloyd's War Medal.

Pacific Grove's war ended on 12th April 1943 in mid-Atlantic. She was homeward bound from New York to Glasgow in convoy HX 232 with a general cargo which included 1,500 tons of diesel oil and four US-built S160 class 2-8-0 locomotives which, after a spell on British railways, were destined to help liberate Europe. Convoy HX 232 was first aware of U-boat activity during the afternoon of 11th April and, after dark, star shells were fired by the escort which encouraged Pacific Grove's master, Captain Pritchard, to order

his crew to 'action stations'. Just after midnight, whilst making 9½ knots, she was struck in the engine room by a torpedo fired by U 563. The German submarine, commanded with some dash, had slipped between an escorting destroyer and a corvette, fired at Pacific Grove, turned and fired at two other ships, Reardon Smith's Fresno City (7,261/1942) and the Dutch Ulysses (2,666/1918). On Pacific Grove the engines stopped immediately, the lights went out, and the deep tank, which was filled with diesel oil, caught fire. As it exploded the torpedo destroyed the two starboard boats, which had been swung out, and - due to some mishandling - the

port boats drifted away before they were full, and the remainder of the crew either jumped into the water or took to the rafts. From the crew of 65 and 16 passengers there were 11 casualties, of whom four were in the engine room and were probably killed outright. Pacific Grove sank after about four and a half hours, and at daylight those in the boats and rafts were picked up by the Flower class corvette HMS Azalea, which also had on board survivors from Fresno City and Ulysses. All were landed at Greenock on 15th April 1943.

The lower photograph is dated 4th August 1934.

PACIFIC EXPORTER (1) (top and middle)

Blythswood Shipbuilding Co. Ltd., Glasgow; 1928, 6,723gt, 436 feet

Two Harland Burmeister & Wain oil engines 8-cyl. 4SCSA by J.G. Kincaid and Co. Ltd., Glasgow driving twin screws; 4,200 BHP, 13 knots

Initially registered in the ownership of Gulf Line Ltd., in 1929 *Pacific Exporter* passed to another Furness Withy subsidiary, Norfolk and North American Steamship Co. Ltd., but this made no difference to her service.

Pacific Exporter remained on the Pacific run until February 1941, then moved to the Atlantic until Operation 'Torch', the North African landings in November 1942. The wartime photograph shows that windows at the forward end of the bridge deck had been plated over. Surviving the war, *Pacific Exporter* was sold to owners in Genoa in 1951, becoming *Giacomo C.* She was broken up in 1958. *[Middle: National Maritime Museum G3977]*

PACIFIC RANGER (1) (bottom)

Burmeister & Wain's Maskin og Skibsbyggeri, Copenhagen; 1929, 6,866gt, 436 feet

Oil engines 8-cyl. 4SCSA by A/S Burmeister & Wain's Maskin og Skibsbyggeri, Copenhagen driving twin screws; 4,200 BHP, 13 knots

Seen here on 25th February 1939, *Pacific Ranger* was the second war loss from this group. On 12th October 1940 she became a victim of *U 59* after dispersing from convoy HX77 whilst on a voyage from Seattle to Manchester with metals, lumber and general cargo. All her crew got away safely in three boats. Captain Evans' boat was found on 21st October by the Icelandic long liner *Thormodur* (101/1919), another was sighted by an RAF aircraft on October 18 and picked up by HMS *Antelope*. The third landed at Belmullet, Eire on 18th October.

PACIFIC IMPORTER (top)

California Shipbuilding Corporation, Los Angeles, California; 1943, 7,259gt, 423 feet
T. 3-cyl. by Joshua Hendy Iron Works, Sunnyvale, California; 2,500 IHP, 11 knots.

In 1947 four Liberties were bought to act as a stop gap until new ships could be built to replace war losses. *Pacific Importer* had been launched as *John Tipton*, but was completed for bareboat charter to the Ministry of War Transport as *Samtredy*, management being given to Prince Line. Unlike other British liner companies, Furness quite rapidly disposed of its Liberties, and *Pacific Importer* went to Italian owners in 1953 to become *Aquitania*. New York-based Greeks bought her 1965, but as *Ayia Marina* she was arrested for debt at Rio de Janeiro in 1969, and sold for breaking up there later that year.

    A juicy bit of trivia: in April 1950 *Pacific Importer* returned to her native California to load 646 tons of raisins, the first imported into the UK since 1939. *[Ian Farquhar collection]*

SAMCALIA and **PACIFIC LIBERTY**
(opposite middle and bottom)
California Shipbuilding Corporation, Los Angeles, California; 1943, 7,258gt, 423 feet
T. 3-cyl. by Joshua Hendy Iron Works, Sunnyvale, California; 2,500 IHP, 11 knots.
Prior to their sale, all four Liberties had been managed on behalf of the Ministry of War Transport by Furness Group companies. Launched as *Lorrin A. Thurston*, the *Pacific Liberty* had been the *Samcalia* until 1947, managed by Furness, Withy and Co. Ltd. - their funnel colours are apparent on the photograph opposite. On the sale of *Pacific Liberty* in 1954, Genoese owners renamed her *Phoebus*, transferring her to a Liberian subsidiary as *Bayhorse* in 1962. Final owners were Swiss-based, although registered in Panama, and as *San Gabriel* she was broken up at Split early in 1971. [Both: Ian Farquhar collection]

SAMAVON and **PACIFIC NOMAD**
(this page top and middle)
New England Shipbuilding Corporation, Portland, Maine; 1943, 7,290gt, 423 feet
T. 3-cyl. by Vulcan Iron Works, Wilkes-Barre, Pennsylvania; 2,500 IHP, 11 knots.
Launched as *Bronson Alcott*, but quickly renamed *Samavon*, on purchase in April 1947 she became *Pacific Nomad*, an excellent name for a tramp, and it was ironic that it was given to a cargo liner plodding a set route. She did go tramping after Furness sold her in 1954, however, first as the Embiricos-owned *Nikolos*, and after 1960 as the *Stamatis*. Her end came on 3rd November 1966 when she dragged her anchors in a cyclone off Madras, where she was waiting to load wheat for Calcutta. Further damage eight days later saw her declared a constructive total loss and sold for scrap. [Both: John Hill collection]

PACIFIC RANGER (2) (bottom)
New England Shipbuilding Corporation, Portland, Maine; 1943, 7,282gt, 423 feet
Harrisburg Machinery Cotrporation, Springfield, Massachusetts; 2,500 IHP, 11 knots
Not all the Liberties bareboat chartered to the Ministry of War Transport were

launched with typical Liberty names, and *Samdaring* was so called from new. Photographed on 24th January 1948, *Pacific Ranger* was to be the first of the Liberties sold by Furness, going in 1952 to Lemos and Pateras who renamed her *San Dimitris*. In 1958, Italian owners bought her, and as *Priaruggia* she was involved in one of those odd bits of ship surgery which, generally, did little to prolong the lives of Liberties. In 1960 her forepart was joined at Genoa with the afterpart of sister ship *Albaro* (8,481/1943), the resulting ship being named *Albaro*. Quite what this expensive operation was meant to achieve is obscure, as her Italian owners sold her after just three years. As the Greek flag *Aigaion* she lasted until 1968 when she was broken up at Osaka. [Ian Farquhar collection]

PACIFIC STRONGHOLD (1) (top and middle)
*Bethlehem-Fairfield Shipyard Inc.,
Baltimore, Maryland; 1945, 7,698gt, 439 feet
Geared steam turbines by Westinghouse
Electric and Manufacturing Co., Pittsburgh,
Pennsylvania; 6,000 SHP, 15.5 knots.*
The only Victory type in the North Pacific
fleet was originally the *Tusculum Victory*,
one of only twelve bought by British owners,
Furness also taking *Stamford Victory*
(7,681/1945) which became *British Prince*.
After seven years as *Pacific Stronghold*, she
was transferred to Prince Line in 1954 as
Malayan Prince.

Sale by Prince Line in 1959 brought
a series of flag-of-convenience owners
whose naming schemes seem intended to
preserve anonymity, and in the space of just
eleven years she was known as *Wang
Knight, Marine Carrier, Elie V, Oceanic Wave*,
and *Silver Falcon*. She arrived at Kaohsiung
for demolition on 21st January 1970.

In the top photograph, in charterer's
colours, *Pacific Stronghold* has an extension
to her funnel not apparent in the middle view.
*[Top: Fotoflite incorporating Skyfotos,
courtesy Peter Kenyon]*

PACIFIC FORTUNE (bottom and opposite top)
*Blythswood Shipbuilding Co. Ltd., Glasgow;
1948, 9,400gt, 499 feet
Parsons geared steam turbines by John
Brown and Co. Ltd., Clydebank; 7,700 SHP,
15.5 knots.*
Having been an all-motorship fleet pre-war,
starting with *Pacific Fortune* turbines were
specified for initial post-war newbuildings.
This at least simplified the post-war career
of *Pacific Fortune*, as few flag-of-
convenience owners could be bothered with
their complexity. C.Y. Tung - who was later to
buy the Furness Group - was clearly not
allergic to turbines, and buying the ship in
1965 ran her as *Malaysia Fortune* until she
was delivered to Taiwanese breakers on 15th
May 1974. On this page *Pacific Fortune* is
seen on the Thames in charterer's colours.
[This page: Peter Kenyon collection]

PACIFIC UNITY

Sir J. Laing and Sons Ltd., Sunderland; 1948, 9,511gt, 499 feet
Geared steam turbines by Parsons Marine Steam Turbine Co. Ltd., Wallsend-on-Tyne; 7,700 SHP, 15.5 knots
The initial letters of the names of the post-war fleet spelled out F U R N E S - unfortunately, an S was missing. Second in the sequence, *Pacific Unity* was actually the first to go in 1964. New owners were N. and J. Vlassopulos who placed her under the Liberian flag as *Lavrentios.* She arrived at Shanghai in April 1970 and was broken up in August by the grandly if slightly misleadingly titled China National Machinery Import and Export Corporation.
[Fotoflite incorporating Skyfotos, courtesy Peter Kenyon]

PACIFIC RELIANCE (2) (top and middle)
Vickers-Armstrongs Ltd., Newcastle-on-Tyne;
1951, 9,442gt, 501 feet
Geared steam turbines by Parsons Marine
Steam Turbine Co. Ltd., Wallsend-on-Tyne;
8,470 SHP, 15.5 knots
Post-war Furness ships were a development
of pre-war designs, and again, twelve
passengers were carried, and there was
130,000 cubic feet of reefer space.

    Pacific Reliance had the honour of
spending her (relatively short) life under one
name and, more or less, one owner. In 1970
she was transferred to Royal Mail Lines Ltd., a
Furness company, but was not renamed,
because she was on the disposal list. She
was photographed in Royal Mail colours on
23rd May 1970 (middle). On 26 March 1971
she arrived at Bruges for demolition.

PACIFIC NORTHWEST (opposite bottom)
Vickers-Armstrongs Ltd., Newcastle-on-Tyne; 1954, 9,442gt, 501 feet
Geared steam turbines by Parsons Marine Steam Turbine Co. Ltd., Wallsend-on-Tyne; 8,470 SHP, 15.5 knots
Pacific Northwest had the melancholy distinction of making the last North Pacific Line sailing, arriving in London in May 1971. She then joined the fleet of Papalios' Aegis Shipping, and as *Aegis Power* was broken up at Shanghai in 1974. [*Fotoflite incorporating Skyfotos, courtesy Peter Kenyon*]

PACIFIC ENVOY (upper)
Vickers-Armstrongs Ltd., Newcastle-on-Tyne; 1958, 9,439gt, 501 feet

Geared steam turbines by Parsons Marine Steam Turbine Co. Ltd., Wallsend-on-Tyne; 8,470 SHP, 15.5 knots
The last two of the postwar newbuildings, *Pacific Envoy* and *Pacific Stronghold*, had 162,000 cubic feet of reefer capacity compared with the 130,000 cubic feet of the earlier vessels. As a result of the Furness' acquisition of Royal Mail, *Pacific Envoy* (seen here in 1966) spent the years 1967 to 1970 running in Royal Mail colours as *Loch Ryan*. Ironically, only when renamed *Pacific Envoy* in 1970 was ownership formally transferred to Royal Mail Lines Ltd. This was merely a preliminary to sale, however, in a deal which saw Aegis Shipping acquire most of the *Pacifics*, and she became *Aegis*

Strength. Chinese mainland shipbreakers took her in 1974, and she was last reported lying off Whampoa awaiting demolition in March.

PACIFIC STRONGHOLD (2) (lower)
Vickers-Armstrongs Ltd., Newcastle-on-Tyne; 1958, 9,439gt, 501 feet
Geared steam turbines by Parsons Marine Steam Turbine Co. Ltd., Wallsend-on-Tyne; 8,470 SHP, 15.5 knots
When sold in 1971, *Pacific Stronghold* took the same route as her running mates, becoming *Aegis Honor* under the Greek flag. She must have met up with the former *Pacific Envoy* at the end, as both were demolished at Whampoa in March 1974.

PACIFIC EXPORTER (2) as **ARAMAIC** (top), **OROPESA** (middle), and **LANTAO ISLAND** (bottom)

Bremer Vulkan, Schiffbau und Maschinenfabrik, Vegesack; 1957, 6,553gt, 475 feet

MAN oil engines by Bremer Vulkan, Schiffbau und Maschinenfabrik, Vegesack; 10,100 BHP, 17.5 knots

The final pair of *Pacific* boats had a slightly more complex history. *Pacific Exporter* was built for joint Shaw Savill and Furness Withy ownership as *Aramaic*. In 1968 she was transferred to the Pacific Steam fleet as *Oropesa*, becoming *Pacific Exporter* very briefly in 1970, without change of registered ownership and apparently being rather camera shy under this name. Reverting to *Oropesa* later that year, she was sold in 1972 to the Hong Kong Islands Shipping Co. Ltd. who renamed her *Lantao Island*. After a further ten years' service, the motorship was broken up in Taiwan in late 1982.

PACIFIC RANGER (2) as **ARABIC** (upper) and **LAMMA ISLAND** (lower)
Bremer Vulkan, Schiffbau und Maschinenfabrik, Vegesack; 1956, 6,553gt, 475 feet
MAN oil engines by Bremer Vulkan,

Schiffbau und Maschinenfabrik, Vegesack; 10,100 BHP, 17.5 knots
The two handsome, German-built, non-refrigerated motorships had careers which ran in absolute parallel, almost until their end. The *Pacific Ranger* was

originally *Arabic*, became Pacific Steam's *Oroya*, and reverted to this in 1971 after just a year as *Pacific Ranger*. Her final name, *Lamma Island*, was carried from 1972 until broken up at Inchon, Korea in 1983.

The _Panmure_ at Port Adelaide, South Australia, at the end of one of her emigrant passages. The cook poses outside his galley and five members of the crew put a tight harbour stow on the fore royal, under the gaze of a couple of shore spectators. Whips have been rigged between the masts to discharge cargo and the passengers' baggage, and an awning has been spread over the poop. The portholes pierced in the half-round of the poop mark the first-class passenger accommodation. _[Maritime Museum of Monterey, Capt. Walter Frederick Lee Collection]_

140

PRIDE AND FALL - THE PANMURE
John Naylon

There is a sadness attending the last days of any vessel, but there seems to be a particular poignancy about pictures of old sailing ships going to the breakers - not only wearied with hard weather, age and painful economies but also leaving a world which no longer had any use for their kind. This is especially true of vessels which were once among the aristocrats of the seas. The photographs of the *Panmure* which accompany this article record a typical trajectory of the last days of sail - from the British to the German and then to the Norwegian flag - and also depict a decline from first-class emigrant clipper to worn-out drudge.

The Dundee Clipper Line

Basil Lubbock states that among the finest of the iron clippers which took emigrants to Australia and New Zealand in the 1870s and 1880s were the 1,500-ton sister ships of David Bruce's Dundee Clipper Line. In 1875 Messrs. A. Stephen and Sons, long known as builders of Dundee whalers, launched five full-riggers for the company: the *Airlie*, *Camperdown* and *Panmure* at Glasgow, and the *Duntrune* and *Maulesden* at Dundee. All were good carriers and powerful vessels, with a good turn of speed in strong winds, and for cabin passengers

provided handsomely-fitted saloons with polished oak panels, bronze ornamentation, balustrades and columns, and tinted tiles. At the height of the emigration boom to New Zealand and Queensland they carried up to 500 steerage passengers in their 'tween decks. In the 'eighties, under the pressure of competition from steam, passenger rates to Brisbane were extraordinarily low: only £5 for steerage and £15 for second cabin.

Of the five sister ships the *Maulesden* had the best reputation for speed: in 1876 she ran out to Otago in 72 days and in 1887-8 went from London to Sydney in 74 days, but her best performance was in 1884 when she sailed from Greenock to Maryborough, Queensland, in 69 days - a record never beaten or even approached. The *Duntrune* also could show her heels: in 1887 she went from Port

Her emigrant days over, and now a general trader, the *Panmure* lies at anchor in San Francisco bay, her sails sent down, awaiting a grain cargo. There is still a plentiful provision of lifeboats, from her passenger days, and the master's going-ashore gig hangs in the falls. Denoting her changed status, the jibboom has been shortened to the outer jib band and the fore royal and topgallant stays brought in accordingly. [San Francisco Maritime National Historical Park, Fireman's Fund, SCR 3b.P13-B]

Augusta to Valparaiso in 31 days and in 1895 from Prawle Point to Mebourne in 74 days; and the *Camperdown* took 400 emigrants from London to Nelson in 80 days in 1876. The *Panmure*, on the other hand, does not seem to have done anything out of the ordinary: Henry Brett in *White Wings* records that in 1878 she arrived in Port Chalmers, New Zealand, under Captain Downie with 29 passengers in the fairly leisurely time of 99 days.

The *Panmure* under the Red Ensign

The *Panmure* and her sisters were named after localities or estates around Dundee. Launched in June 1875 she measured 1,581 tons gross and 1,505 tons net on dimensions 246.6 x 38.3 x 23.3 feet, with a 40-foot poop and a 37-foot forecastle. The usual voyage of Bruce's clippers was with emigrants to the Antipodes, across to the Bay of Bengal, and then home to Dundee with Calcutta jute; eventually, however, they were forced into tramping. The *Panmure* seems to have led an uneventful life, apart from stranding on 27th July 1891 off Salt River, Table Bay, Cape Colony while on passage with coal from Barry Dock towards Cape Town under Captain J. Hughes. Even at this late date she carried a substantial crew of 31. This incident may explain why Lubbock, in *The Last of the Windjammers*, Volume I, records her as 'wrecked August 4, 1891'; in fact the iron hull had another 32 years of life in it.

Sold to Germany

In 1893 the *Panmure* was sold to Christian Michael Matzen of Hamburg and renamed *Vasco da Gama*. Matzen owned a fleet of 17 barques and one full-rigger (the ex-*Panmure*) between the 1870s and his death in 1904, including some notable vessels

Pictured here under the German flag as the *Vasco da Gama* (below), the ex-*Panmure* shows her vintage in her courses clewing up to the bunt and her lower topsails to the quarters, instead of to the yardarms as in later vessels. [Dr. Jürgen Meyer collection]

Towing into what may be a South American port (above), the *Hermanos* still retains an air of breeding; but the long jibboom of her palmy days has entirely gone, leaving just the short spike of her original bowsprit. The standing spanker gaff has been removed and a monkey gaff has been rigged at the mizzen crosstrees for signalling purposes. [National Maritime Museum P3648]

such as the *Edith*, ex-*Star of Persia* (1,264/1868). Under Captain J. Jestrum the former emigrant clipper now traded to Brazil, Oregon, Australia and Chile, and showed what she could do when driven in the German style, going from the Lizard to Antofagasta in 71 days in 1903-4. When Matzen died after 40 years of shipowning his fleet was dispersed, the last vessels to be disposed of being the steel barque *Cap Horn*, ex-*Nithsdale* (1,683/1896), sold along with the *Vasco da Gama* to Norway in 1905, the well-known steel barque *Emin Pasha* (1,617/1890), also sold in 1905 to Knöhr und Burchard of Hamburg, and the iron barque *Gudrun* (1,476/1886), which went to August Bolten of Hamburg in 1906.

Last days under the Norwegian flag

Initially the *Vasco da Gama* became the *Hermanos,* owned by Akties. Hermanos of Lillesand and managed by Henr. Hansen, who ran a fleet of seven sailing vessels and one steamer. In 1911 she became the *Dova Rio*, owned by Akties. Dova Rio (manager D.A. Knudsen of Söndre Hyggen, Röken) and in this guise had a notable running mate in the shape of the iron barque *Dova Lisboa* (1,492/1885), formerly the *Cambrian Chieftain* of Liverpool. The *Cambrian Chieftain* featured in an heroic rescue off the west coast of South America in December 1894. On passage from Newcastle, New South Wales to Valparaiso she was thrown on to her beam ends in a full gale and all her boats were carried away. In this condition she was found by the barque *Dee* (1,169/1885), which rescued 14 of her complement at the cost of the lives of the second mate and four men of the *Dee*. The *Cambrian Chieftain* was eventually got into Coquinbo by her master Captain Thomas and the remainder of his crew.

The names *Dova Rio* and *Dova Lisboa* imply an engagement in Portuguese-Brazilian trade and enlightenment here would be welcome. In any event the two ships must have earned handsome freights as neutrals during the First World War; but the coming of peace and the collapse of freight rates meant the end, as for so many of the world's remaining deep-water sailing ships. At the end of the war both vessels, still classed 100A1 at Lloyds, passed under the management of Harald Wellen of Christiania, and from his hands to the breakers in 1923-4.

The end of the trail

In 1923 the *Dova Rio*, by now reduced to barque rig, was brought into the small port of Watchet, Somerset, and moored alongside the western breakwater. During 1923-4 she was gradually reduced to scrap by the Cardiff Marine Stores Company, a shipbreaking concern which had the exclusive use of Watchet West Pier and the berths alongside, for which it paid Watchet Council £90 per year plus £20 for each vessel broken up. In 1925 the firm itself ran into financial difficulties and ceased operations at Watchet. The *Dova Lisboa*, ex-*Cambrian Chieftain*, was broken up during 1924-5 at Sunderland, the port where she had been launched in 1885.

With just a skeleton crew aboard, the *Dova Rio* is led into her last berth at Watchet in 1923. Although now reduced to barque rig, the tell-tale position of the mizzen top indicates that she was once a full-rigger. The standing spanker gaff has been restored. Topgallant masts have been sent down and boats, sails and other items of value have been removed, although the spare sheet anchor is still lashed in its original position against the break of the forecastle. The permanently rigged awning rails on the poop may be confirmation of her engagement in trade to South America. *[Author's collection]*

The Lamport and Holt Vs
Rowan Hackman

The Vs were the most splendid collection of liners Lamport and Holt owned during their long history.

William James Lamport always prided himself on being born on the day Wellington won the Battle of Waterloo. In 1845, at the age of thirty, he went into partnership with a young man of twenty years of age, George Holt, whose brother Alfred later became famous as the founder of the Blue Funnel Line. Lamport himself came from a shipowning and shipbuilding family which lived on the coast of the county which has now reverted to its ancient name of Cumbria. The two partners, until 1860, owned a number of sailing ships, which traded world-wide, although most of their passages were either across the Atlantic to North or South America, or to the Far East and Australia, apart from which there was the occasional voyage to the Mediterranean or South Africa. Their first ship was the barque *Christabel*, launched at Workington on 17th September 1845. She was of 335 tons, but after a few voyages was sold, to be replaced by other notable ship- and barque-rigged vessels including the *Cathaya*, launched at the newly-opened Lamport yard at Workington on 26th April 1850, as Yard No. 2.

Astronomers to inventors

For some years, like so many of their contemporaries, the two partners were doubtful about going into steam. However, after purchasing a small steamship which they renamed *Zulu* (189/1857) - but which was soon sold as being too small - they ordered two steamships, one from Scott's yard at Greenock, and the other from Andrew Leslie at Hebburn-on-Tyne. The 1,210gt *Memnon*, launched by Scotts on 28th March 1861, gave them many years of useful service, but the second steamer, *Copernicus* (1,597/1861), was sold to French buyers who had made an offer which they could not refuse. Under the name *Copernic* she served her new owners for more than thirty years. For the next few years the partners added more sailing ships to their fleet, and it was not until 1865 that they were persuaded to establish the Liverpool, Brazil and River Plate Steam Navigation Co. Ltd., and to order four more steamers from Andrew Leslie. Their first steamships were all named after astronomers, and this was possibly due to the fact that astronomy, as a result of watching the many spectacular comets of the nineteenth century, was enjoying as much attention in the eyes of the public as dinosaurs have enjoyed recently. The great comets of 1808, 1811, and 1843, and the reappearance of Halley's Comet in 1836, were followed by the large comet discovered by the Italian astronomer Donati in March 1858, which remained visible all through the following winter. I can remember my grandmother telling me how she, at the age of six, was taken out to see it. The next great comet appeared in 1882, and my father told me how he could see its nucleus overhead, while the tail disappeared below the horizon, when his father took him, at the age of nine, out into their garden to see it.

However, as the Lamport and Holt fleet rapidly expanded, the supply of astronomers' names gave out, and so dramatists, poets, artists, sculptors, philosophers, and inventors were all added to the list, the names of the fleet covering the whole of western European history from *Homer*, *Thales*, *Plato* and *Virgil*, to *Wordsworth*, *Tennyson*, *Browning*, *Rossetti*, and *Chantrey*; some being used several times. Politicians were conspicuous by being few in number, only *Canning*, *Chatham* and *Cavour* meriting this distinction. In 1868 the company was awarded a postal contract by the Brazilian Government, and the following year commenced, in a somewhat irregular fashion, trading to New York from Buenos Aires with cargoes of coffee.

William James Lamport died suddenly in 1874 at the early age of 59, leaving his partner to continue the business, to which he added new partners amongst whom was Walter Holland, who had always been interested in trade with South America. At the same time, the failure of the Ryde Line with its service from Antwerp to South America led to the company forming the Société de Navigation Royale Belgique to take over this service and to which eight of its ships were transferred, flying the Belgian flag and registered at Antwerp. The service was to last until 1908.

In 1898 the occasional voyage from Buenos Aires to New York developed into a regular service, carrying passengers and live cattle from the Argentine, as well as coffee from Brazil. The pioneer ships on the service were the new Rs: *Raphael* (4,699/1898), *Romney* (4,464/1898), *Rembrandt* (4,667/1899), *Raeburn* (6,511/1900) and *Rossetti* (6,508/1900). They were followed in 1899 and 1900 by the sisters *Calderon* (4,083/1900) and *Camoens* (4,070/1900), and with the older *Canning* (5,366/1896), *Canova* (4,637/1895), *Cervantes* (4,635/1895) and *Cavour* (4,914/1895) occasionally joining them. In 1901 and 1902 the smaller T class were placed on the service, the *Thespis* (4,343/1901), *Terence* (4,309/1902), *Tintoretto* (4,181/1902), and *Titian* (4,70/1902).

The regular service between Buenos Aires, Montevideo, Santos, Rio de Janeiro and New York was now proving to be such an unqualified success that larger ships were needed, although two Furness vessels, which had proved too large for their intended service, the clipper-bowed *Evangeline* and *Loyalist*, were added under the names of *Tennyson* (3,901/1900) and *Byron* (3,909/1901). So out came the first of the splendid Vs. The first to arrive was the *Veronese*, from Workman, Clark and Co. of Belfast in January 1906, and followed by the *Velasquez* from Sir Raylton, Dixon and Co. at Middlesbrough, delivered on 20th February 1906. The same year two more were ordered, the 20-feet longer *Voltaire* from D. and W.

The Lamport and Holt Vs were a group only in so far as their names and, to an extent, their trades were concerned - they were by no means a class. The Belfast-built *Veronese* (top) and the short-lived *Velasquez* (middle) were sisters but the Clyde-built *Voltaire* (1) (below) was 20 feet longer and significantly more powerful, albeit similar in layout. *[Middle: Peter Newall collection]*

Henderson on the Clyde, and from Workman, Clark at Belfast the somewhat smaller *Verdi*. Of the Vs, the *Verdi* was the only ship not used on the Buenos Aires to New York route, spending the whole of her career on the Liverpool to Buenos Aires service. She had been launched as the *Trajan*, but was renamed before delivery in December 1907. In 1908 the *Vasari* was ordered from Sir Raylton, Dixon and Co. She was of a similar length to *Voltaire* but had a different hull form and a capacity for a total of 580 passengers.

Peacetime losses

In thick fog on 16th October 1908 while bound to New York from Buenos Aires *Velasquez* struck the rocks at San Sebastiao, near Santos, and became a total loss, although fortunately without loss of life. The company's steamer *Milton* (2,679/1888) arrived from Santos to help rescue the crew and passengers to find that they had safely reached the shore in the ship's boats. They were picked up from the beach by *Milton*, which also salvaged their cabin baggage. All attempts to salvage the *Velasquez* failed, and there was a similarity between her loss and that of the Royal Mail Lines' *Magdalena* (17,547/1949) on the same coast in 1949. On completion, the *Vasari* took the place of *Velasquez*, and was the first of the group to be propelled by quadruple-expansion engines.

In 1910 further Vs were ordered, all from Workman, Clark: the sisters *Vandyck*, *Vauban* and *Vestris*, larger again than the *Vasari*, and all driven by quadruple-expansion engines. Before they were completed, control of the company had passed to their great rivals, the Royal Mail Steam Packet Company, and Owen Cosby Phillipps, later Lord Kylsant, had become chairman. In spite of this, the two companies continued to operate as separate entities, although *Vauban* was briefly owned by Royal Mail as *Alcala* in 1913. It is interesting to note that the later Vs resembled closely their rivals, the D class of Royal Mail (see *Record* 12), but one can scarcely say that they were as fortunate.

Before war came in 1914 the *Veronese* had also been lost. Sailing from Liverpool on 12th January 1913, she carried 97 crew and 20 passengers. She sailed from Vigo for Buenos Aires on 15th January 1913, having embarked a further 97 Spanish and Portugese emigrants for South America. In darkness and heavy seas on the following morning, she struck the Boa Nova Rocks two miles north of Leixoes. One lifeboat was launched, but capsized in the heavy seas with the loss of 43 lives. Lifeboats from shore could not approach the wreck because of the heavy seas but, as *Veronese* lay right under the cliffs, the remaining passengers and crew were winched ashore by breeches buoy. Captain Service was the last to leave his ship, just before 3.00 pm.

War losses

Three of the Vs were sunk by enemy action, two by surface raiders. On 26th October 1914, *Vandyck* was intercepted by the light cruiser SMS *Karlsruhe* whilst on a voyage from Buenos Aires to New York. All the 410 persons aboard were transferred to a German cargo ship, *Asuncion* (4,663/1894), whilst *Vandyck* was used by the Germans as a tender and scout, along with six other captured British ships: *Bowes Castle* (4,650/1913), *Condor* (3,053/1893), *Highland Hope* (5,159/1903), *Hurstdale* (2,752/1902), *Indrani* (5,706/1912), and *Strathroy* (4,336/1909). On 31st October, *Asuncion* was sent into Para with the prisoners, whilst the other ships were scuttled. *Vandyck* proved to be *Karlsruhe*'s last victim.

Just over two years later, *Voltaire* was also sunk by a German raider, the famous SMS *Moewe*, which had been built in 1914 for F. Laiesz as the reefer *Pungo* (4,500/1914). Converted to a raider, she was placed under the command of Count von und zu Dohna-Schlodien. She sailed on her first cruise in January 1916, and before her return to Kiel at the end of February had succeeded in sinking ten British vessels. *Moewe* sailed on her second cruise from Kiel on 23rd November 1916, and on 2nd December the *Voltaire* became her first victim, sunk in the Atlantic with her entire complement being taken prisoner. During the remainder of *Moewe*'s second cruise she sank ships off the coasts of Canada, Brazil, and Portugal before returning to Kiel northwards of the British Isles, showing how an innocent reefer can be turned into a formidable raider. After the war she was handed over to the United Kingdom and became the *Greenbrier* in the fleet of Elders and Fyffes.

On 21st August 1917, *Vasari* was missed by a torpedo from U 53, but the submarine made up for this disappointment by sinking the *Verdi* the next day. *Vestris* was also missed by a torpedo in the English Channel on 26th January 1918. The *Vauban* seems to have been the luckiest, as no attack by enemy craft of any kind is recorded

Postwar replacements

As soon as they were released from military service following the end of the First World War, *Vasari, Vauban*, and *Vestris* were chartered to Cunard. The service for which the Vs had been built - Liverpool to New York and Buenos Aires - was maintained by smaller vessels, including the attractive

Vasari in the dazzle paint which may well have helped her to avoid a torpedo from U 53 in August 1917, allowing her to go on to have by far the longest life of the Vs (see page 150). Of a similar length to *Voltaire*, the Middlesbrough-built *Vasari* had extensive passenger accommodation. One publication claims she was built to replace *Velasquez*, but as she was launched just seven weeks after the latter came to grief, if true Richardson, Westgarth must have built exceedingly quickly.
[National Maritime Museum P17298]

Vandyck (1) (top), Vauban (middle) and Vestris (see page 152) were sisters, enlarged versions of Vasari, representing a substantial order for their Belfast builder.

With control of Lamport and Holt having recently passed to Lord Kylsant, Vauban was sold to the Royal Mail Steam Packet Company when she was scarce eight months old and renamed Alcala. The claim in another publication that this was merely a charter is discounted by an entry recording change of ownership in the vessel's closed register. She reverted to Vauban and Lamport and Holt ownership in December 1913. [Top and middle: Peter Newall collection; bottom: A.S. Pope collection]

little *Byron* (3,909/1901) and *Tennyson* (3,944/1900) which became firm favourites with US travellers.

New ships were needed, and orders were placed with Workman, Clark for two larger vessels which took the names of their predecessors which had been sunk by enemy raiders, *Vandyck* and *Voltaire*. The first to be launched, in February 1921, was *Vandyck*, a twin-screw ship driven by steam turbines. At the time of *Vandyck*'s launch, her sister ship, *Voltaire*, had been expected to take the water in April or May, but the completion and the launch of the respective sisters were both delayed because *Vandyck*'s turbines suffered excessive vibration. Although this problem was eventually resolved, it was decided to give the *Voltaire* quadruple-expansion engines and this considerably delayed her completion. On delivery *Vandyck* was chartered by the Cunard and Royal Mail Lines, and so it was not until 1924 that both sisters finally entered the service for which they had been ordered. The three pre-war Vs shared service with them.

But this all ended with the tragic loss of the *Vestris* on 12th November 1928. Having arrived from London, she left New York on the 9th for Buenos Aires, with 129 passengers and a crew of 150. On the morning of 12th November an SOS was received from her, in position some 400 miles off Hampton Roads, saying that she was sinking. She was abandoned at 1.22 pm, all passengers and crew taking to the lifeboats in heavy seas. The first ship to arrive on the scene was the *American Shipper* (7,430/1921) of United States Lines, but by then some of the boats had been overwhelmed and with them 112 lives lost. The exact cause of the leak was never established, but it may have been caused by the *Vestris* striking some wreckage.

The loss of the *Vestris* followed that of the Italian liner *Principessa Mafalda* (9,210/1908) off the Brazilian coast the previous year. This had been caused by the propellor shaft fracturing and piercing the hull, and was also accompanied by heavy loss of life. Together, these losses led to the New York to Buenos Aires service collapsing. The two older Vs were laid up. The *Vauban*, having been the most fortunate of the group during the war in avoiding enemy attack, was sold to breakers in 1931. The *Vasari* long outlived all her sisters. In 1929 she was sold to become a fish factory ship and in 1935 was sold to Sovtorgflot in the same capacity. In 1960 she was deleted from *Lloyd's Register*, but in February

1979 surprised shipping enthusiasts by arriving at Kaohsiung, having been sold to Taiwanese breakers after a career of 70 years.

Cruising and cruisers

After the collapse of the service, the company was left with two splendid ships, which it seemed entirely undecided how to employ, and until late 1932 both were laid up off Netley in Southampton Water. Eventually, the growing popularity of cruising prompted the company to use them for Mediterranean cruises. So, late in 1932, the two sisters were handed over to Harland and Wolff, who completely refurbished them. This included giving them white hulls, a distinctive feature of all cruising liners of that time, including the famous old *Mauretania* (30,696/1907). From 1933 until the outbreak of war in 1939 the sisters spent the summers cruising and the winters laid up. The *Voltaire* arrived back at Liverpool after her first cruise on 4th April 1933, whilst the *Vandyck* arrived at Liverpool on 1st July after refitting in Southampton, and sailed three days later on her first Mediterranean cruise.

When war was declared in 1939, the sisters were just finishing their cruising for the year and the Admiralty quickly took them up with a view to converting them to armed merchant cruisers, which had proved so successful between 1914 and 1918. However, neither ship proved adequate for this type of work, probably because they were rather smaller than others used in this role. Instead the *Vandyck* became an accommodation ship at Scapa Flow. Her end came in 1940 when she was sent to assist in the evacuation of Narvik. She was bombed and set ablaze off Harstad on 9th June, and finally sank two days later. Nearly all her complement escaped to the shore where they were taken prisoner by the Germans.

Voltaire survived her sister only by ten months, and after a more chequered spell of service. After trooping to Bombay, she too was briefly sent to Scapa Flow, but was then fully armed as an escort for convoys. She spent most of 1940 as an inspection ship in the Mediterranean, but was then based at Freetown in Sierra Leone to escort convoys across the Atlantic to Halifax. Returning from one of these trips she was attacked by the German commerce raider, *Thor*, on 9th April 1941. After a fight that lasted nearly two hours she was abandoned in sinking condition. Out of complement of 272 men, 75 were killed and the remainder taken prisoner.

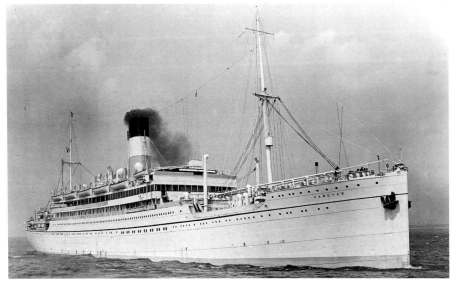

Vandyck (2) looked splendid in white.

Veronese wrecked at Leixoes in January 1913 (top).

VERONESE 1906-1913
O.N. 120912 7,022g 4,510n 465.0 x 59.2 x 29.9 feet
T. 3-cyl. by Workman, Clark and Co. Ltd., Belfast; 660 NHP, 3,300 IHP, 11½ knots.
14.11.1905: Launched by Workman, Clark and Co. Ltd., Belfast (Yard No. 228).
8.1.1906: Registered in the ownership of the Liverpool, Brazil and River Plate Steam Navigation Co. Ltd. (Lamport and Holt Ltd., managers), Liverpool as VERONESE.
9.1.1906: Completed.
28.1.1906: Left on maiden voyage from Liverpool to Buenos Aires.
16.1.1913: Wrecked two miles north of Leixoes, Portugal whilst on a voyage from the Clyde and Liverpool to Rio de Janeiro and the River Plate with general cargo. A total of 43 lives were lost.
1.2.1913: Register closed.

VELASQUEZ 1906-1908
O.N. 120921 6,988g 4,452n 465.0 x 59.3 x 29.9 feet
T. 3-cyl. by Richardsons, Westgarth and Co. Ltd., Middlesbrough; 660 NHP, 3,300 IHP, 11½ knots.
9.12.1905: Launched by Sir Raylton, Dixon and Co. Ltd., Middlesbrough (Yard No. 518).
20.2.1906: Completed and registered in the ownership of the Liverpool, Brazil and River Plate Steam Navigation Co. Ltd. (Lamport and Holt Ltd., managers), Liverpool as VELASQUEZ.
18.3.1906: Left on maiden voyage from Liverpool to Buenos Aires.
16.10.1908: Wrecked at San Sebastiao, Santos whilst on a voyage from Buenos Aires to New York with general cargo.
27.11.1908: Register closed.

VOLTAIRE (1) 1907-1916
O.N. 124049 8,406g 5,500n 485.3 x 58.2 x 34.1 feet
T. 3-cyl. by D. and W. Henderson and Co., Glasgow; 780 NHP, 4,500 IHP, 13 knots.
31.1.1907: Launched by D. and W. Henderson and Co., Glasgow (Yard No. 456).
13.3.1907: Registered in the ownership of the Liverpool, Brazil and River Plate Steam Navigation Co. Ltd. (Lamport and Holt Ltd., managers), Liverpool as VOLTAIRE.
16.3.1907: Completed.
31.3.1907: Left on maiden voyage from Liverpool to Buenos Aires.
2.12.1916: Captured and scuttled by the German auxiliary cruiser SMS MOEWE 650 miles west by a quarter north of Fastnet whilst on a voyage from Liverpool to New York in ballast.
13.3.1917: Register closed.

VERDI 1907-1917
O.N. 124103 6,578g 4,180n 430.4 x 53.3 x 28.8 feet
Passengers: 100 first, 100 second, 350 third.
T. 3-cyl. by Workman, Clark and Co. Ltd., Belfast; 714 NHP, 3,850 IHP, 12¾ knots.
23.10.1907: Launched by Workman, Clark and Co. Ltd., Belfast (Yard No. 256) as TRAJAN.
12.12.1907: Registered in the ownership of the Liverpool, Brazil and River Plate Steam Navigation Co. Ltd. (Lamport and Holt Ltd., managers), Liverpool as VERDI.
18.12.1907: Completed.
1.1908: Left on maiden voyage direct to New York.
22.8.1917: Torpedoed and sunk by the German submarine U 53 115 miles north west by west of Eagle Island in position 55.17 north by 12.58 west whilst on a voyage from New York to Liverpool.
29.8.1917: Register closed.

Verdi (right) was something of an odd-man-out in this group. She had no sisters, never served New York, and was the smallest of the Vs despite having accommodation for 550 passengers. Indeed, her intended name *Trajan* suggests that she was not conceived as part of the group. *[Peter Newall collection]*

Above is an early view of *Vasari,* taken before deckhouses were added alongside the foremast. Below she is in Hellyer ownership as the fish factory *Arctic Queen.* [Both: Peter Newall collection]

VASARI 1909-1928

O.N. 127974 8,401g 5,277n 486.0 x 59.3 x 27.4 feet
Passengers: 250 first, 130 second, 200 third.
T. 3-cyl. by Richardsons, Westgarth and Co. Ltd., Middlesbrough; 754 NHP, 4,100 IHP, 12³/4 knots.
8.12.1908: Launched by Sir Raylton, Dixon and Co. Ltd., Middlesbrough (Yard No. 518).
22.4.1909: Completed.
28.4.1909: Registered in the ownership of the Liverpool, Brazil and River Plate Steam Navigation Co. Ltd. (Lamport and Holt Ltd., managers), Liverpool as VASARI.
9.5.1909: Left on maiden voyage from Plymouth to New York and Buenos Aires.
7.3.1928: Sold to Hellyer Brothers Ltd., Hull.
27.3.1928: Renamed ARCTIC QUEEN on conversion to a fish factory ship.
7.1935: Sold to Sovtorgflot, Russia and renamed PISCHEVAYA INDUSTRIYA.
2.1979: Arrived at Hong Kong en route to Kaohsiung for demolition.

VANDYCK (1) 1911-1914

O.N. 131378 9,862g 6,219n 495.5 x 60.8 x 28.7 feet
Passengers: 280 first, 130 second, 200 third.
Q. 4-cyl. by Workman, Clark and Co. Ltd., Belfast; 1,096 NHP, 6,500 IHP, 14¹/2 knots.
2.6.1911: Launched by Workman, Clark and Co. Ltd., Belfast (Yard No. 301).
4.9.1911: Registered in the ownership of the Liverpool, Brazil and River Plate Steam Navigation Co. Ltd. (Lamport and Holt Ltd., managers), Liverpool as VANDYCK.
7.9.1911: Completed.
5.10.1911: Left on maiden voyage from Liverpool to Buenos Aires.
26.10.1914: Captured by the German auxiliary cruiser SMS KARLSRUHE 690 miles west by south of St. Paul's Rocks in position 01.14 south by 40.40 west whilst on a voyage from La Plata to New York with general cargo.
31.10.1914: Scuttled off Para, Brazil after being used as a scout and tender.
9.12.1914: Register closed.

VAUBAN 1912-1932

O.N. 131432 10,421g 6,537n 495.5 x 60.8 x 28.7 feet
Passengers: 280 first, 130 second, 200 third.
Q. 4-cyl. by Workman, Clark and Co. Ltd., Belfast; 1,100
NHP, 6,500 IHP, 14½ knots.
19.1.1912: Launched by Workman, Clark and Co. Ltd.,
Belfast (Yard No. 302).
20.4.1912: Registered in the ownership of the Liverpool,
Brazil and River Plate Steam Navigation Co. Ltd.
(Lamport and Holt Ltd., managers), Liverpool as
VAUBAN.
23.4.1912: Completed.
4.5.1912: Left on maiden voyage from Liverpool to

Buenos Aires.
14.3.1913: Owners became the Royal Mail Steam Packet
Company, London.
1.4.1913: Renamed ALCALA.
25.11.1913: Owners became the Liverpool, Brazil and
River Plate Steam Navigation Co. Ltd. (Lamport and Holt
Ltd., managers), Liverpool.
11.6.1914: Renamed VAUBAN.
1928: Laid up.
1931: Sold to T.W. Ward Ltd., Sheffield.
25.1.1932: Arrived at Pembroke for demolition at Milford
Haven.
26.7.1934: Register closed.

Sisters *Vandyck* (1) (above) and *Vauban* (below).

This photograph of *Vestris* was taken on 4th January 1913, and purports to show her on her maiden voyage. However, the date 19th September 1912, given in the fleet list below, seems more likely given that she was completed earlier that September: perhaps the above shows her return from her maiden voyage. It was the loss of *Vestris* in 1928 that led to the abandonment of the New York to Buenos Aires service of Lamport and Holt. *[Peter Newall collection]*

VESTRIS 1912-1928

O.N. 131451   10,494g 6,623n   495.5 x 60.8 x 28.7 feet
Passengers: 280 first, 130 second, 200 third.
Q. 4-cyl. by Workman, Clark and Co. Ltd., Belfast; 1,096 NHP, 6,500 IHP, 14½ knots.
16.5.1912: Launched by Workman, Clark and Co. Ltd., Belfast (Yard No. 301).
24.8.1912: Registered in the ownership of the Liverpool, Brazil and River Plate Steam Navigation Co. Ltd. (Lamport and Holt Ltd., managers), Liverpool as VESTRIS.
3.9.1912: Completed.
19.9.1912: Left on maiden voyage from Liverpool to Buenos Aires.
12.11.1928: Foundered after springing a leak in position 37.25 north by 70.33 west whilst on a voyage from London and New York to Buenos Aires. A total of 112 lives were lost.
28.11.1928: Register closed.

VANDYCK (2) 1921-1940

O.N. 145876   13,233g 7,960n   510.6 x 64.3 x 39.3 feet
Passengers: 300 first, 150 second, 230 third.
Steam turbines by Workman, Clark and Co. Ltd., Belfast; 7,000 SHP, driving twin screws, 14 knots.
24.2.1921: Launched by Workman, Clark and Co. Ltd., Belfast (Yard No. 359).
21.9.1921: Completed and registered in the ownership of the Liverpool, Brazil and River Plate Steam Navigation Co. Ltd. (Lamport and Holt Ltd., managers), Liverpool as VANDYCK.
27.9.1921: Left on maiden voyage to New York and the River Plate.
28.6.1934: Owners became the Lamport and Holt Line Ltd., Liverpool.
9.6.1940: Bombed and set on fire by German aircraft off Harstad, near Narvik and abandoned the next day, although she was further attacked on 11.6.1940. Seven members of her crew were lost, others got ashore and 161 were taken prisoner.
18.4.1946: Register closed.

Vandyck (2) as a cruise ship.

VOLTAIRE (2) 1923-1941

O.N. 147238 13,248g 7,997n 510.5 x 64.3 x 39.3 feet
Passengers: 300 first, 150 second, 230 third.
Two Q. 4-cyl. by Workman, Clark and Co. Ltd., Belfast;
1,544 NHP, 8,000 IHP, 14½ knots.
14.8.1923: Launched by Workman, Clark and Co. Ltd.,
Belfast (Yard No. 360).
6.11.1923: Registered in the ownership of the Liverpool,
Brazil and River Plate Steam Navigation Co. Ltd.
(Lamport and Holt Ltd., managers), Liverpool as
VOLTAIRE.
23.11.23: Completed.
25.11.1923: Left on maiden voyage from Liverpool to

New York and South America.
28.6.1934: Owners became the Lamport and Holt Line
Ltd., Liverpool.
11.1939: Converted on the River Tyne to an Armed
Merchant Cruiser, armed with eight 6 inch guns and
renamed HMS VOLTAIRE.
4.4.1941: Sank following an engagement with the German
auxiliary cruiser SMS THOR in the North Atlantic in position
14.30 north by 40.30 west whilst on a voyage from Halifax to
Trinidad and Freetown as a convoy escort. Of her crew, 75
were killed and 197 survivors were taken aboard *Thor.*
18.4.1946: Register closed.

Two views of *Voltaire* as a cruise ship in the Mersey. In these shots, and in that of *Vandyck* (2) opposite, a flag is flown at the foremast and as a stem jack which appears to carry the arms of the city of Liverpool. There must be a story to this!

CHANNEL VISION

The files of Fotoflite have some superb views of older ships, taken on sweeps of the English Channel by Skyfotos 'planes in the 1950s and 1960s. Here are four of the visions they captured of ships of an earlier age.

HENRY WARD (above)
William Beardmore and Co. Ltd., Coatbridge; 1923, 1,509gt, 267 feet
T. 6-cyl. by William Beardmore and Co. Ltd., Coatbridge driving twin screws.
Henry Ward was one of the unsung heroes of the London River, dumping at sea the end product of sewage treatment. Built for the London County Council, she worked on well into the twilight years of the steamship, arriving at Antwerp for breaking up on 28th January 1964 in tow of the *Bulldog II*. As most major British rivers had them, it is perhaps surprising that noone, as far as is known, has published a comprehensive history of the sludge carrier.

The General Steam motor vessel in the background is *Hirondelle* (757/1950). Despite the title of this feature, this photo was probably taken in the Thames Estuary and not the English Channel.

TUCANA (below)
Barclay, Curle and Co. Ltd., Glasgow; 1928, 3,824gt, 330 feet
T. 3-cyl. by Barclay, Curle and Co. Ltd., Glasgow.
The rather exotic funnel design of Eric K.C. Hornemann of Lübeck helps disguise a British cargo liner from between the wars. The extralarge bridge house and its awnings helps identify her as the former *Lafian*, delivered to the African and Eastern Trade Corporation Ltd., which was shortly to become the United Africa Co. Ltd., predecessors of the Palm Line. *Lafian* never took a Palm name, being sold in 1936 to Moss Hutchison who renamed her *Meroe*.

Sale to Germany came in 1950, and she initially took the name *Adele*, in 1957 becoming *Tucana* for just one year, which neatly dates this photograph. She was to have a further Lubeck owner as *Ursula* before she passed to Far Eastern buyers, becoming in quick succession *Mien An*, *Ruhamah*, and *Liby*, being broken up at Hong Kong in 1968.

TASSOS (above)

Lithgows Ltd., Port Glasgow; 1930, 5,316gt, 421 feet

Oil engine 4SCSA 8-cyl. by J.G. Kincaid and Co. Ltd., Greenock.

Tassos has featured in *Record* before, but this fine view shows off the large bridge structure which accommodated 25 passengers. The first reference to her in *Record* was in issue 1, where she was shown under her original name of *Tolten* when managed by Trinder, Anderson and Co. Her career was somewhat tortuous, and letters from Bill Laxon and John B. Hill in *Record* 2 were necessary before it could be sorted out.

Tolten was built for the Compania Sud-Americana de Vapores of Valparaiso but was sold back to her builders in 1932 when the Chilean owners got into financial difficulties. She later sailed as *Glenearn* for Glen Line. As Bill Laxon explained, subsequent registration in the name of Trinder, Anderson and Co. was a cover for actual ownership by the Union Steam Ship Co. of New Zealand Ltd. who wished to run her with an Indian crew. In 1942 she was sold to the South American Saint Line Ltd., who renamed her *St. Merriel* in 1945. She found further employment as *Helios* under the Finnish flag, and in 1959 became *Tassos* as seen here. Owners were the Santa Irini Shipping Co. Ltd., of Monrovia, but she was put under the then-fashionable Lebanese flag. As her name *Tassos* suggests, her real owner was Greek, one Emmanuel A. Karavias, who entrusted her management to the Nomikos family in London.

Tassos arrived at Hong Kong for breaking up in April 1967 after a long and varied career.

NADIR (above)

Prince Rupert Dry Dock Co. Ltd., Vancouver; 1945, 7,160gt, 425 feet

T. 3-cyl. by the Dominion Engineering Works Ltd., Montreal.

Although a relative youngster compared with the other ships featured here, *Nadir* shows some interesting features in this aerial view, not least the deck cargo of timber which has all but submerged the derricks. This cargo raises two questions: the timbers are the right length for pitprops, but were these still used in the 1960s when this photograph must have been taken, or is it merely timber sawn to convenient lengths for pulp mills?. And secondly, with every inch of available deck space used, presumably the crew had to climb over the timber to move around the ship?

Nadir was completed as *Elgin Park*, having been launched as *Fort Simcoe*, so could claim the honour of being both a Fort and a Park. After the war she was quickly bought by a Canadian subsidiary of Furness, Withy and given the Prince Line name *Royal Prince*. In 1949 she became the *Atlantic Star*, owned as her name suggests by the Livanos family. Owner when photographed was Faik Zeren of Istanbul for whom presumably the name did not have the meaning of 'low point' it has in English. Zeren kept her until 1971 when she was broken up at Eregli, Turkey.

It would be interesting to know how long her appearance had differed from that of other Forts and Parks. The bridge is distinctly different, with boats removed and the space they occupied partly enclosed. The ventilators alongside the mast houses are also non-standard. Despite these changes, some original features remain, including the gun tubs on the bridge wings. The latter suggests that she was built this way, or modified before the ending of the war removed the need for gun tubs.

HANSEN SHIPBUILDING, BIDEFORD Part 2
Roy Fenton and Michael Guegan

The first Hansen-built steamer, *Hubbastone* in Cumberland Basin, Bristol on 6th June 1938. *[Graham Farr]*

1. HUBBASTONE   1921-1940
O.N. 145131   873g 431n   190.0 x 30.1 x 12.6 feet
T. 3-cyl. by the Lytham Shipbuilding and Engineering Co.
Ltd., Lytham; 51 NHP, 550 IHP, 9 knots.
15.10.1920: Launched.
1.1921: Completed.
10.1.1921: Registered in the ownership of the Hansen
Shipping Co. Ltd. (Hansen Brothers Ltd., managers),
Cardiff as HUBBASTONE.
5.11.1924: Sold by mortgagees to S. and R. Steamships
Ltd. (Thomas Stone and Joseph Rolfe, trading as Stone and
Rolfe Ltd., managers), Llanelli.
23.5.1940: Damaged by German aircraft and abandoned in
sinking condition in dock at Dieppe, where she had
discharged a cargo of coal from Swansea. The crew of 12
were saved.   She was refloated by the Germans and
renamed JURGENSBY.
6.1943: Sunk in the Baltic.

2. MONKSTONE (1)   1921-1958
O.N. 145179   873g 431n   190.0 x 30.1 x 12.5 feet
T. 3-cyl. by the Lytham Shipbuilding and Engineering Co.
Ltd., Lytham; 51 NHP.
1.1921: Launched.
4.1921: Completed for the Hansen Shipping Co. Ltd. (Hansen
Brothers Ltd., managers), Cardiff as MONKSTONE.
1922: Sold to Richard Hughes and Co., Liverpool and
renamed WILD ROSE.
20.4.1934: Owners became. Richard Hughes and Co.
(Liverpool) Ltd. (Thomas J. Tierney, manager), Liverpool.
2.4.1941: Beached near Rosslare Harbour following an air
attack twelve miles south east of the Tuskar Rock whilst on
a voyage from Dublin to Cardiff.   Refloated, towed to
Dublin and later repaired and returned to sevice.
1951: Sold to George W. Grace and Co. Ltd., London and
renamed SUSSEX ELM.

1953: Sold to the Holderness Steamship Co. Ltd., Hull and
renamed HOLDERNENE.
19.2.1958: Arrived at Dublin for breaking up by the
Hammond Lane Foundry Ltd.

3. STEVENSTONE   1921
O.N. 146044   873g 437n   190.0 x 30.1 x 12.5 feet
T. 3-cyl. by the Lytham Shipbuilding and Engineering Co.
Ltd., Lytham; 51 NHP, 550 IHP, 9 knots.
9.7.1921: Launched.
8.1921: Completed.
16.8.1921: Registered in the ownership of the Hansen
Shipping Co. Ltd. (Hansen Brothers Ltd., managers),
Cardiff as STEVENSTONE.
12.1921: Left Appledore on her maiden voyage.
16.12.1921: Left Blyth for Elsinore with a cargo of coal
and disappeared.
1.2.1922: Posted missing.
8.2.1922: Register closed.

4. STURDEE ROSE   1922-1945
O.N. 145983   873g 443n   190.0 x 30.1 x 12.5 feet
T. 3-cyl. by the Lytham Shipbuilding and Engineering Co.
Ltd., Lytham; 84 NHP, 550 IHP, 9¾ knots.
27.5.1922: Launched.
10.1922: Completed.
21.10.1922: Registered in the ownership of Richard
Hughes and Co., Liverpool as STURDEE ROSE.
20.4.1934: Owners became Richard Hughes and Co.
(Liverpool) Ltd. (Thomas J. Tierney, manager), Liverpool.
16.11.1945: Capsized and sank off Trevose Head whilst on
a voyage from Garston to Plymouth with a cargo of coal.
Eight of her crew of twelve were lost; the survivors being
picked up eight days later by the steamer TECUMSEH
PARK (7,163/1943).
18.12.1945: Register closed.

Hansen yard number 2 as *Wild Rose* (upper left), *Sussex Elm* (upper right), and *Holdernene* (bottom left). Yard number 4, *Sturdee Rose*, is seen bottom right [*World Ship Photo Library Cochrane collection*].

5. RUNNELSTONE 1923-1961

O.N. 146685 869g 427n 190.0 x 30.1 x 12.5 feet
T. 3-cyl. by MacColl and Pollock Ltd., Sunderland; 99 NHP.
1922: Launched.
1.1923: Completed for the Hansen Shipping Co. Ltd. (Hansen Brothers Ltd., managers), Cardiff as RUNNELSTONE.
1924: Sold to the S. and R. Steamships Ltd. (Stone and Rolfe, managers), Llanelli.
1946: Sold to R.H. Penney and Sons, Shoreham and

renamed ALGEIBA.
1954: Sold to John S. Monks and Co. Ltd., Liverpool and renamed FOAMVILLE.
21.3.1961: Whilst on a voyage from Manchester to Ireland in collision near the Northwich Road Swing Bridge, Stockton Heath, Warrington with the steam hopper MARY P. COOPER (953/1896) which sank. Taken to Manchester for dry docking and declared a constructive total loss.
4.5.1961: Arrived at Preston for breaking up by T.W. Ward Ltd.

Yard number 5 seen (top) as the Shoreham-owned *Algeiba* and (bottom) as Monks' *Foamville*. Under the latter name she became infamous for her part in a collision which largely blocked the Manchester Ship Canal for three weeks. In the aftermath of the incident she was

photographed waiting to be broken up at Preston. *[Top: World Ship Photo Library]*

Yard number 6 became the second *Monkstone*, seen opposite top with a cargo of barrels. Confusingly, like the first *Monkstone* she also took the name *Sussex*

Elm in later life. Close comparison of the two confirms that the *Sussex Elm* seen opposite bottom is yard number 6. *[Roy Fenton collection and Fotoflite incorporating Skyfotos]*

6. MONKSTONE (2)   1923-1946
O.N. 147484   867g   425n   190.0 x 30.1 x 12.5 feet
T. 3-cyl. by the Lytham Shipbuilding and Engineering Co.
Ltd., Lytham; 84 NHP, 550 IHP, 9½ knots.
25.2.1923: Launched.
5.1923: Completed.
15.5.1923: Registered in the ownership of the Hansen
Shipping Co. Ltd. (Hansen Brothers Ltd., managers),
Cardiff as MONKSTONE.
5.11.1924: Sold by mortgagees, National Provincial Bank
Ltd., to S. and R. Steamships Ltd. (Stone and Rolfe Ltd.,
managers), Llanelli.
19.12.1941: Sold to George W. Grace and Co., London.

4.3.1946: Owners became George W. Grace and Co. Ltd.,
London.
10.10.1946: Renamed SUSSEX ELM.
26.7.1951: Sold to the Bristol Steam Navigation Co. Ltd.,
Bristol.
2.8.1951: Renamed SAPPHO.
23.6.1953: Sold to the Williamstown Shipping Co. Ltd.
(Comben, Longstaff and Co. Ltd., managers), London.
26.6.1953: Renamed KENTBROOK.
4.2.1954: Wrecked three miles north of Orfordness
Lighthouse whilst on a voyage from Ipswich to Goole in
ballast. Declared a constructive total loss.
1.4.1954: Register closed.

7. WHEATHILL   1923-1955

O.N. 145735   265g   96n   127.0 x 22.1 x 7.8 feet
C. 2-cyl. by William Beardmore and Co. Ltd., Coatbridge, Glasgow; 72 NHP.
7.1923: Launched.
11.1923: Completed for Spillers Steamship Co. Ltd., Cardiff as WHEATHILL.
2.6.1926: Owners moved to Liverpool
25.2.1927: Owners became Spillers Milling and Associated Industries Ltd., London.
5.12.1927: Owners became Spillers Ltd., London
1933: Sold to J.R. Watt and Sons Ltd., Portrush and renamed RATHMORE.
1935: Sold to William A. Leith, Aberdeen.
1937: Owners became George Couper and Co. Ltd., Helmsdale and renamed RIMSDALE.
1942: Managers became Duncan and Jamieson Ltd.
1944: Managers became Bloomfields Ltd. (Coastal Shipping Department).
1947: Owner became C.B. Simpson, Aberdeen.
1948: Sold to the Mac Shipping Co. Ltd., Glasgow and renamed COMALA.
1952: Manager became Thomas J. Metcalf, London.
22.10.1955: Arrived at Port Glasgow for breaking up by Smith and Houston Ltd.

8. WHEATBLADE   1923-1955

O.N. 145730   265g   96n   127.0 x 22.1 x 7.8 feet
C. 2-cyl. by William Beardmore and Co. Ltd., Coatbridge, Glasgow; 72 NHP.
6.1923: Launched.
9.1923: Completed for Spillers Steamship Co. Ltd., Cardiff as WHEATBLADE.
2.6.1926: Owners moved to Liverpool
25.2.1927: Owners became Spillers Milling and Associated Industries Ltd., London.
5.12.1927: Owners became Spillers Ltd., London
1933: Sold to A.F. Henry and MacGregor Ltd., Leith and renamed DENWICK HEAD.

Wheathill, seen below at Preston, was one of two smaller coasters built by Hansen.

1946: Sold to the Lochbroom Trading Co. Ltd., Inverness (Bloomfields Ltd. (Coastal Shipping Department), Aberdeen, managers) and renamed MOREFIELD.
1948: Sold to the Mac Shipping Co. Ltd., Glasgow.
1952: Manager became Thomas J. Metcalf, London.
7.7.1955: Arrived at Port Glasgow for breaking up by Smith and Houston Ltd.

9. WHEATCROP   1924-1956

O.N. 145737   523g   199n   162.0 x 25.6 x 9.9 feet
C. 2-cyl. by William Beardmore and Co. Ltd., Coatbridge, Glasgow; 99 NHP.
29.9.1923: Launched.
1.1924: Completed for Spillers Steamship Co. Ltd., Cardiff as WHEATCROP.
2.6.1926: Owners moved to Liverpool
25.2.1927: Owners became Spillers Milling and Associated Industries Ltd., London.
5.12.1927: Owners became Spillers Ltd., London
1952: Sold to John S. Monks and Co. Ltd., Liverpool.
1953: Renamed ROCKVILLE.
18.7.1956: Arrived at Barrow for breaking up by T.W. Ward Ltd.

10. WHEATPLAIN   1924-1930

O.N. 145744   523g   199n   162.0 x 25.6 x 9.9 feet
C. 2-cyl. by William Beardmore and Co. Ltd., Coatbridge, Glasgow; 99 NHP, 650 IHP, 9½ knots.
27.11.1923: Launched.
3.1924: Completed.
10.3.1924: Registered in the ownership of Spillers Steamship Co. Ltd., Cardiff as WHEATPLAIN.
2.6.1926: Owners moved to Liverpool
25.2.1927: Owners became Spillers Milling and Associated Industries Ltd., London.
5.12.1927: Owners became Spillers Ltd., London
27.3.1930: Wrecked on Tory Island, County Donegal whilst on a voyage from Birkenhead to Westport with a cargo of flour.
27.3.1930: Register closed.

After almost 20 years with Spillers, *Wheatcrop* (above) was sold to Monks in 1953 to become the second of their three ships to be named *Rockville* (below).

[Bottom: David Hocquard]

HELP PUT IT ON RECORD

In this column we ask readers to help us locate elusive photographs or information to complete features planned for future issues of *Record*. Your help will make *Record* even more of a record.

Between 1912 and 1914, Glasgow shipowner John Paton had 18 small motor coasters built at various Scottish yards. All had names beginning *Innis-*, which ran through the alphabet from *Innisagra* to *Innisvera*. The fleet was quickly scattered, and photographs are very rare: we know only of views of *Innishannon* and *Innisulva*, the latter being reproduced on page 105 of *Record* 14. Later names carried by these craft included *Eva Petersen*, *Ben Olliver*, *Stratton Croft*, and *Truro Trader*. Can a reader help us locate photographs of these wee coasters under any name?

As mentioned in the letters column, a photograph of the C1-M-AV1 *Jutahy* is sought under this name.

Has anyone photographs of casualties to, or unusual incidents involving Clan Liners?

We are also looking for anyone with information on London freighter owners Buries Markes Ltd., associates of French grain traders Louis Dreyfus.

Lastly, do we have anyone knowledgeable about Spanish ships who would be willing to read the histories of some Spanish cargo steamers and attempt to add a little background on their trades and ownership?

GUAN GUAN AND THE GOLDEN LIBERTIES
Captain A.W. Kinghorn

By the middle of the nineteen sixties the famous US-built Ocean and Liberty ships and their Canadian and British-built contemporaries, the Forts, Parks and Empires, were coming to the ends of their surprisingly long lives. Surprising, because when they were built it was considered they would, with luck, see the war out, with little future thereafter; while many were still earning their owners good freights in the early nineteen sixties. But now, twenty years after that war, hulls *were* wearing out and their anachronistic engines were increasingly expensive to run and maintain. However, the dry cargo they pursued had not yet succumbed to containerisation or complete takeover by the giant bulker. There was still plenty of work for the versatile general cargo carrier with 'tween deck and own derricks which would enable her to work her cargo in and out at ports which did not yet have the facilities to do so themselves. Many small ports around the world did not see the need to spend their limited resources on dockside cranes when the ships using them possessed their own adequate gear. Better to spend the cash on dredging their channels and on deepwater basins, to permit larger cargoes to come and go safely. So - when the war-built vessels came to the end of their days - what to do?

A place for the 'tween decker

An economical replacement of around 15,000 tonnes deadweight carrying capacity seemed to be the answer, with a 'tween deck through her four or five hatches, economically propelled by an internal combustion engine running on the cheapest oil fuel and able to drive her along at around 15 knots, rigged with the most useful outfit of derricks, manned by a total complement of, say, 35 men.

Whereas a full homogenous bulk cargo does not need a 'tween deck - indeed frowns upon it as an internal deck impedes grab discharge - a mixed general cargo requires that extra deck space below the upper deck on which to stow parcels of timber and structural steel including piping, cases of machinery, cartons of glassware and medical equipment, bales of cloth, bags of lampblack, sacks of beans, drums of carbide and essential oils - to name but a few items. There are some low-value general cargoes which even today do not justify the enormous expense of containerisation. Smaller bulk parcels of dense chrome ores are best stowed partly in the 'tween decks and mostly in the lower hold to give a ship comfortable stability. There remains - perhaps always will - a need for ships able to carry such commodities - mostly around what we in the west call the Third World. These ships were just the kind Guan Guan needed.

The Japanese designed and built several types of five-hatch Liberty-replacements, and a class called the MM14 which had only four holds but was of similar dimensions and carrying capacity. These latter, while never numerous, continued to be built into the late seventies. By this time the Americans

had - perhaps temporarily - gone out of merchant shipbuilding. Britain came up with the Sunderland SD14 - a very popular class - while the Germans dispensed with class lettering to design and build what they simply called the Liberty Replacement.

Built originally for German owners, most of these ships passed after a few years to Far Eastern buyers, notably the Chinese who operated them under their own proliferating 'private' companies wearing a variety of funnel colours, registered in Chinese ports and Chinese manned. Communist China must be the only nation today operating a vast merchant fleet entirely under her own yellow-starred red ensign, manned throughout by her own people. That Chinese wages remain remarkably low accounts for this, of course.

Two of this Liberty Replacement class which I had the honour to command in their later years, while they sailed under Singapore ownership and flag, were the *Golden Harvest* (9,221/1970) and *Golden Bear* (9,338/1970). Built by Rickmers of Bremerhaven as *Irmgard Jacob*, and by Flensburg Schiffbau Gesellschaft on the Baltic as *Martha Fisser,* respectively, they were bought by the Singapore private family shipowners Guan Guan in 1986 for little more than scrap prices. At this time they lay in Hong Kong, where they had been laid-up for some time with consequent deterioration. But the Thio family who owned Guan Guan recognised a brace of good ships when they saw one. They were prepared to spend money to bring them up to scratch and, as with all their fleet, each vessel was registered as a separate company in ancient time-honoured custom - to defray liabilities if they ever occurred.

The Golden Line

Guan Guan - the Golden Line - had been founded by Mr K. L. Thio who, born around 1918 in Nam Chin, Hokien, China, was a long-time resident as part of the Chinese ethnic minority in Indonesia. An astute and very hardworking man (his motto was 'No day is a holiday'), he had built up a prosperous business in exporting local produce and saw opportunities in the newly-emerging nation's struggle for freedom from the colonial Dutch. The Europeans had returned in the wake of the defeated Japanese invaders in 1945, intending to resume colonial rule over what had for three centuries been known as the Dutch East Indies. But the Indonesians had other ideas and a bitter war for independence ensued. A fleet of small Thio-owned ships, commanded and manned by Indonesians, replaced the Dutch vessels which with their predecessors had dominated those waters for centuries (and now lay sunk in Tanjung Priok and other Indonesian ports, their rusting masts, funnels and upperworks protruding above the shallow water). Thio's fleet built up a steady inter-island trade, boosting the new nation's economy. As this prospered in those golden years, ownership expanded, Thio buying always second- or third-hand

One of Thio's earliest passenger vessels, *Kim Ann* was built by Bartram, Sunderland for Companhia Nacional de Navegacao of Portugal as *Timor*. Despite her modest size, the routes served by *Timor* and her sister *India* (which became Guan Guan's *Kim Hock*) were lengthy; from Lisbon through the Suez Canal then either east to Macao and Timor or south to Mozambique an Angola. Guan Guan acquired this neat twin-screw motorship in 1974, but her end is uncertain: *Lloyd's Register* deleted her in 1985.

Kim Hwa was better known as *Daressa*, last of four D-class motorships built for British India's mail service between Bombay and the Persian Gulf. She was built with accommodation for 86 berthed passengers and a massive 659 deck passengers, and had refrigerated space in her holds. The Barclay, Curle-built *Daressa* was the first of the group to be sold, buyers being part of the Chandris group who renamed her *Favorita* in 1964. Guan Guan bought her in 1968 whilst she was laid up at Piraeus, and renamed her *Kim Hwa* for a service between Penang and Swatow. She was sold to Hong Kong breakers in July 1974.

ships, never new ones. During the mid 'fifties he purchased the ex-British India liner *Kistna* (1,465/1924), renaming her *Giang Bee* and putting her on a new cargo-passenger service between Singapore and Indonesia. He always preferred his ships to run as liners rather than to follow the uncertain work of tramping.

But the new, dictatorial Indonesian government coveted the growing wealth of their resident Chinese and began a form of what is now known as ethnic cleansing. For the good of their health the Thio family removed to Singapore, taking their ships with them and placing them under Singapore registry though still employing largely Indonesian crews. Mr Thio's dream was to own 50 ships trading worldwide. Although it never quite reached this number his fleet grew to well over 40, trading to 25 countries, including Europe. Now that they were based in Singapore, Chinese Singaporeans were employed as ships' officers, none more important in those days than the Chin Chew, the owner's representative afloat who passed on the owner's instructions to the British captain about ports and cargo, including orders where to go next. This was how Singapore companies operated. As the years rolled by the fleet expanded steadily. By acquiring more modern tonnage as the older vessels were displaced, Thio expanded into the passenger liner trades, buying a couple of Portuguese ships, the *India* (7,631/1951) and *Timor* (7,656/1951) which he renamed *Kim Hock* and *Kim Ann* respectively. Capable of carrying 300 passengers each, this pair operated a passenger cargo service between Singapore, Malaysian ports and China. When

western nations, led by the USA, refused to trade with Communist China, the fact that Guan Guan continued to do so stood the company in good stead for the future. The Chinese appreciate loyalty and in the years to come Guan Guan were one of only two non-communist foreign lines allowed to operate a cargo liner service - loading valuable general on a monthly basis in China for Colombo, Karachi and ports in the Persian Gulf. The other company was the German Rickmers, which to this day runs a liner container service between China and Europe.

Golden expansions

More vessels purchased during this expansion period included another British India liner, the *Daressa* (5,180/1950) which was renamed *Kim Hwa*. Elder Dempster's *Tamele* (7,173/1945) became *Golden City* in 1967, while Federal Line's *Northumberland* (8,046/1955) became a later *Golden City* in 1972. The John Brown-built *Waipara* (6,414/1956) ex-*Wharanui* was bought and renamed *Golden Lion* in 1971. Booth Line's *Dominic* (3,827/1945) became the *Golden Ocean*, Moller's *Nicoline Maersk* (8,702/1951) became *Golden Jade* while the Dutch-built *Parkhaven* (5,620/1956) was bought and renamed *Golden Horse*. There were at least three *Golden Wonders*. The first, which had been the Kockums-built *Amazonas* (7,332/1943-45), had the distinction of lowering the British ensign for the last time to raise the new white-crescent-with-five-white-stars red ensign of the Republic of Singapore. This little ceremony, carried out with great dignity and maximum press coverage, made her the founder member of the Singapore merchant fleet. This far-

Elder, Dempster's twin-screw motor vessel *Tamele* was bought by Guan Guan in March 1967 and renamed *Golden City* (top). She had been an early part of the programme of replacing Elder, Dempster's war losses, being launched by Cammell, Laird at Birkenhead in August 1944, and always had something of an air of austerity about her. Given her not-enormous accommodation block, she carried the surprising number of 36 passengers. Guan Guan sold *Golden City* to Hong Kong breakers in 1973.

Seen in Singapore in March 1975, origins of the second *Golden City* as a Federal Liner are in no doubt (middle). She was built by John Brown, Clydebank as *Northumberland*, and briefly served as the Greek *Kavo Astrapi* before becoming *Golden City* in 1973. She was broken up at Hong Kong five years later.

Golden Lion (bottom) is clearly out of the same mould as *Golden City*, although a trifle shorter. Another Clydebank product, she was originally New Zealand Shipping's *Wharanui*, transferring within the P&O group to become British India's *Waipara* in 1969. Bought by Guan Guan in 1971, she went to breakers at Kaohsiung in 1979.

The wisdom of perpetuating the split superstructure layout has been debated before in *Record*, and here we have a Danish example of the type (top). Guan Guan's *Golden Jade* was built and engined by Burmeister & Wain in 1951 as *Nicoline Maersk* for A.P. Moller. She was unusual in having three masts, as well as a very full outfit of kingposts. Moller put several of its older ships under flags of convenience in the 1960s and 1970s, and this motorship became simply *Nicoline*. She became *Golden Jade* in 1976, but was broken up at Kaohsiung just three years later.

Guan Guan's fleet was nothing if not cosmopolitan. *Golden Horse* (middle) was built at Alblasserdam in 1956 as *Parkhaven* for N.V. Gebr. Van Uden's Scheepvaart Maatschappij of Rotterdam, and acquired by Guan Guan in 1973. She was broken up at Kaohsiung in 1984.

The first *Golden Wonder* (bottom) was built as *Amazonas*, almost the last of a score of Johnson Line twin-screw motor vessels with counter sterns planned in the late 1920s. Delivered in 1943, *Amazonas* did not sail until the end of the Second World War. She was sold to Guan Guan in 1964, retaining her classic appearance as *Golden Wonder* until 1973 when she left Hong Kong for Whampoa and the breakers.

from-comprehensive list gives an idea of the diversity of the company's ship-buying activities at this time.

Mr Thio died in 1976 aged only 58, deeply mourned by his family and employees who had seen him build up one of the largest and most prosperous Singapore shipping companies from virtually nothing. Ownership and management of the fleet was taken over at first by his widow, then by his grown-up offspring - a young lady and two young men, all English educated - who soon realised that times and trades were changing and that they must trim the size of their fleet to fit in with modern thinking. Never deeply into containerisation, they bought and used some second hand 'boxes', but remained to the end committed to the break bulk concept, where cargo is carried not in containers. By this time the fleet was well known throughout the East, smartly maintained with their black or grey hulls, white superstructure, black-topped blue funnels, with matching blue masts and derricks.

Manning the Goldens

The deep-sea ships were all commanded - Mr Thio's decision - by British masters, who were required to run the ships to the best of their ability, experience and knowledge. Provided they did this without incurring undue expense the company backed them to the hilt. Other British officers were also occasionally employed but at a time when they were in great demand in the expanding merchant fleets of their mother country it had to be a specially-dedicated Eastern Hand (perhaps with an oriental wife) who elected to sail under the rather meagre conditions obtaining in the true Far Eastern shipping companies which Guan Guan typified. Wages were not high, although one's income was boosted by not having to pay British income tax if one spent at least one year out of the UK. There was an end-of-contract bonus but no paid leave ('We pay you to work for us, not go on holiday!') and there were few of the social security benefits obtaining under regular British ownership. But this was, and still is, the Way of the East. Before each year's voyages we all signed Singapore Articles which were an exact copy of the old British Articles,

designed to protect owner and seafaring employee alike. A typical Golden Line ship's company would have a British master, retired and on pension from one of the British liner companies, officers from Indonesia, Burma, China, South Korea, Ghana, Nigeria, Bangladesh (though never from India or Pakistan and only rarely from the Philippines), latterly from Montenegro - and a mixed Indonesian/Burmese crowd of ratings. But the Thios, I found, were kindly, considerate people for whom to work. Not only did they allow my wife to sail with me at any time but they also welcomed my adult son for a voyage in the *Golden Bear* and our eight-year-old granddaughter, who spent ten memorable weeks with us aboard the *Golden Harvest* in 1994.

Golden trades

The fare-paying passenger venture was not a great success but cargo carrying was highly profitable, especially in the years immediately preceding containerisation, which came along in the East gradually from the nineteen seventies. When the Vestey-owned Austasia Line - an eastern offshoot of Blue Star Line - was finally pulling ships out of its Singapore to Australia trades, Guan Guan joined them, to operate a joint service. One of these was *Golden Summer* ex-*Washington* (8,696/1949), a handsome twin-screw Sulzer-engined, six-hatch liner built at Saint Nazaire. I saw her, looking very smart, in Sydney during the early 'sixties.

Occasionally, Guan Guan ships crossed the Tasman to New Zealand on Blue Star work. But Guan Guan's old ships' cargo gear often did not match up to the rigorous standards required by the Australasian port authorities and some passengers complained bitterly when the air conditioning broke down. Centuries of shipborne passengers (those making the passage as opposed to those on pleasure cruising) were coming to an end worldwide anyway - and the company's trade between Singapore and Australia lapsed, although Blue Star (Australia) remained Guan Guan's agents for transhipment cargo.

The history of *Golden Summer* began in 1941, when Chantiers et Ateliers de Saint Nazaire S.A. were told by the German occupiers to build two ships for Hamburg Amerika Linie. Work was not exactly rapid, and it was not until 1949 that one of the hulls was completed for Compagnie Générale Transatlantique as *Washington*. After almost 20 years service, Guan Guan bought and renamed the twin-screw motorship. *Golden Summer* was broken up at Hsinkiang, China in 1974.

The rakish-looking *Golden Haven* was acquired in 1984. She had been built for London and Overseas Freighters Ltd., the UK-based operation of Greeks Rethymnis, Kulukundis and Mavroleon which - until their acquisition of Austin and Pickersgill's shipyard seemed to build their ships almost anywhere but in the UK, *London Advocate* being built by De Schelde at Vlissingen. Sold in 1973 to other Singapore owners as *Singapore Fortune*, she was bought by Golden Line (Private) Ltd. in 1984 and became *Gulden Ilaven*. She was broken up at Alang in 1992.

Nine Golden years

I first joined the *Golden Harvest* anchored in Singapore's Eastern Roads in June 1988, by which time Guan Guan were down to four ships, *Golden Harvest*, *Golden Bear*, *Golden Haven* (10,399/1964) and *Golden Wonder* (10,255/1969), all of which I commanded from time to time over the following nine years. They operated a monthly cargo liner service from Shanghai and other Chinese ports to Colombo, Karachi and the Persian Gulf; loading a bulk cargo, usually urea, for ports back east. Sometimes there was time - before presenting at Shanghai to load on 27th of each month - to take a cross cargo, such as copra from the southern Philippines to Korea, or sugar from Bangkok to Japan, which all added interest for the seafarers and profit for the owners.

Golden Haven was the former *London Advocate*, built by De Schelde in Flushing for London and Overseas Freighters. A typical five-hatch, bridge and engines amidships general trader of her time, she was the last Guan Guan ship with this layout. The *Golden Wonder* (a later model than she who first raised the Singapore ensign) was an MM14, built in Shimonoseki by Mitsubishi, 10,255gt on a length of 151.33 metres. One voyage when crossing from Singapore to Taiwan, her main radio transmitter broke down and, after a period when it was feared she had sunk in the China Sea with all hands, she arrived safely - to be heralded in the world press as the 'Return of the Golden Silence.'

Golden Harvest typified the German Liberties. With an overall length of 139.76 by 21 metres beam, on a gross tonnage of 9,221.75 - later increased to 9,443. Specially strengthened to navigate in ice, she had a bulbous bow, raised forecastle and poop, five cargo holds and an interesting transom stern in which a small open deck led into the galley and crew mess-room (a useful deck, much used for fishing when in port or at anchor). Bridge, accommodation and machinery were aft. Deadweight was 15,000 tonnes. Two masts and a pair of samson posts were rigged with ten SWL 10-ton derricks (5 tons in union purchase) and two 80-ton derricks designed to work in tandem which, with a steel beam, were able to lift 160 tons: useful for

placing long, heavy pieces of cargo in the long No.2 hold. The 10-ton derricks' rig was highly advanced with all topping lifts, runners, guys and schooner guys (between the derrick heads when in union purchase) led to electric winches, all under the hand operation of the winch driver, making for swift, safe and economical working. The main engine was a six-cylinder M.A.N. of 7,800 BHP (5,737 Kw) giving a maximum speed of 16 knots.

The five holds were divided horizontally by a 'tween deck incorporating ingenious steel hatch covers which, raised to form a 'tween deck hopper, dispensed with the shifting boards required to be fitted (at great expense!) before loading bulk grain in tonnage not so fitted. No. 3 hold was a deeptank capable of carrying liquid cargo, or water ballast to give bottom weight for loading or unloading heavy lifts.

Accommodation was provided for a total complement of forty, including two pilots. The master's accommodation, I found, was superior to that in the (quite up-market) SD14, Lamport and Holt's *Browning* (9,324/1979) which I had commanded in 1982 in that - in addition to the usual bedroom, bathroom and large dayroom - I now had a large Captain's Saloon - useful for dealing with the hordes of officials who descended at many of the ports visited. These worthies could be dealt with in appropriate style and comfort without actually letting them into my own 'house.' Officers' accommodation was below on two decks while ratings lived mainly in two berth cabins, with some singles, in the poop.

On the chart of Karachi Approaches my predecessor had pencilled where the best fishing was to be had, six miles south of Manora Head. And that was where I anchored, sometimes for days on end awaiting a berth alongside, while the lads landed fish by the bucketful on our little afterdeck Very tasty!

By 1994 containerisation - particularly as operated by the China Overseas Shipping Corporation (COSCO) - was undercutting freights on general cargo to such a degree that Guan Guan began to call it a day and put their ships up for sale, one by one. *Golden Haven*, the oldest dating from 1964, went first after many years of profitable service, followed by the short-lived *Golden Star* (9,497/1974) - a German Liberty replacement built without bulbous bow and with no raised poop but three heavily-rigged masts. The *Golden Haven* went to Indian breakers at Port Alang (who allegedly put her back into service) while the *Golden Star* went to the Vietnamese as a going concern. I was in command of the *Golden Harvest* as she was put on the market, when interested parties either came themselves or sent their surveyors to inspect. A group of North Koreans looking for a suitable buy in Singapore Eastern Roads came aboard and, meeting my granddaughter, exclaimed -'this must indeed be good safe ship if the captain brings his little girl!' But the Koreans could not raise the needful and we carried on to the Gulf where I eventually signed, on 30th December 1994, the papers which sold her to the Marwan Shipping and Trading Company of Dubai. The new owner, a white-robed Arab gentleman, was so taken with the ship and her name that he simply renamed her *Harvest*.

Golden Bear was as similar to the *Golden Harvest* as two ships built at widely-different yards can be. Almost identical, she sported a stovepipe atop the funnel, only one jumbo derrick instead of two, and her two fibreglass lifeboats were white, not orange. Otherwise the pair were hard to tell apart. As sometimes occurs in two near-identical sisters, however, the *Golden Harvest* always managed an extra knot speed over a voyage, all things being equal. *Golden Bear* was sold in 1996 and renamed *Semba*, registered at that end-of-the-market flag-of-convenience port Kingstown and removed from German Lloyd classification. When purchased by Guan Guan in Hong Kong ten years earlier she had first been renamed *Golden Land* - a name used previously for the Swan Hunter-built *Staholm* (5,520/1954),

A deck cargo of drums on *Golden Bear*. [Author]

Golden Bear with a floating crane alongside in Shanghai. [Author]

purchased in 1972. While still 'new' however, *Golden Land* ran aground in one of the Chinese rivers when the steering failed. Fortunately there was no personal injury and damage was limited to a few steel plates in the bow. But it was felt, perhaps, that this ship had too close an affinity for the land so her name was changed in Singapore, with appropriate ceremony, to *Golden Bear*, another old favourite.

Golden Wonder (10,255/1969) had been built for the Swiss as *Iguape* and placed at first under the Liberian flag, but soon became *Corviglia* of Basle, which rare port of registry could be seen under the paintwork to the end of her days. Unusual for a ship built so recently as 1969, her graceful lines, bulbless nicely curved stem and rounded cruiser stern gave a very pleasing appearance. Excellent accommodation reflected the upmarket tastes of her original owner and she was powered by a Sulzer engine. Her Singapore Chinese chief and second engineers maintained her machinery and engine room in spotless, immaculate condition. Replaced on the mainline service by the *Golden Grace*, the *Golden Wonder* reverted to tramping round the Far East before being sold for scrap.

Silver into Gold

Golden Grace (10,889/1977) - appropriately named - was the last ship owned by Guan Guan, having come from a Liberian flag company who had her as *Trade Grace* - so the name change was quite simple. *Golden Grace* began life at Mitsubishi's Hiroshima yard as the MM14 Liberty replacement *Silveravon* - one of the last ships to be built for the old British Silver Line. With the same bulbless-bow, cruiser-sterned hull as the *Golden Wonder*, she was powered by a five-cylinder Sulzer designed for 17.5 knots originally, though Guan Guan's economical working speed was usually kept to 12.5 or so. She too had a spotless engine room thanks to her Yugoslav chief and second engineers. Her rig was different in that where the *Golden Wonder* had conventional derricks, the *Golden Grace* sported single swinging derricks with an extra heavy derrick on the mainmast able to service hatches 3 and 4. The last voyage I sailed in her was as usual - cargoes loaded at Tianjin, Xingang and Shanghai for the Gulf - but by now the writing was on the wall. More and more good freight cargo was going exclusively in containers - in big boxboats - all we got apart from some steel pipework and machinery was rough general - sacks of dyes, drums of various essential and lubricating oils,

Golden Bear ex-*Martha Fisser* at Singapore on 4th June 1991. She was broken up in 1998 under her seventh name. She had been twice *Martha Fisser* and twice *Sunbaden*, then *Alpamayo*, before a whole run of 'Goldens' - *Golden Amman*, *Golden Land*, and *Golden Bear*, finally becoming *Simba*. *[Alwyn McMillan]*

The third *Golden Wonder*, ex-*Iguape*, ex-*Corviglia* also at Singapore on 4th June 1991. On her sale to Dubai owners in 1995 her name was reduced simply to *Wonder*, but she did not last long, arriving at Alang to be broken up in January 1997. *[Alwyn McMillan]*

dangerous chemicals of all sorts - carefully stowed so as to not adversely affect each other (by causing fire or explosion). Our eastbound cargoes, however, took us to Kota Kinablu and Sandakan in East Malaysia, North Borneo, with a full load of bagged urea from the Gulf port of Al Jubail. Unlike most of our urea cargoes which were used as fertiliser, this superior grade was to be used in the manufacture of glue, to make the veneers and plywoods which now form a large and valuable export from this part of the world. The following voyage took us with fertiliser urea to Bangladesh - Chittagong and the port of Mongla, up the Pussur River, in that vast jungle delta of the Ganges-Brahmaputra known as the Sundarbans.

By now (1997) Guan Guan were down to this one *Golden Grace* - the monthly westbound service requiring four ships being made up with chartered Chinese tonnage. Surveyors from interested prospective buyers from as far afield as Yugoslavia and Canada came to see us, tap at our steelwork with their little hammers and dive down into our double bottom tanks. Her twin cargo hatches seemed to present problems - suitable for containers, they claimed, but not so good for bulk cargoes - until we explained that at least half of each voyage had been spent 'carrying it in bulk' perfectly satisfactorily. Eventually, by the end of 1998, a Malaysian became

seriously interested. By this time this liner trade had ended for break-bulk ships and she was tramping, for instance phosphate from Aqaba to Tuticorin. The Yugoslavs from Montenegro went home as UN sanctions on their own merchant navy lifted. They had proved themselves great shipmates, marvellously dedicated engineers and fine seamen.

The Malaysian gentleman bought the ship, renamed her *Santa Suria* and told her Guan Guan British captain and his entire crew that their jobs with him were safely assured. The Thio family, having made a comfortable living from their ships over the last 45 years, were not interested in joining the hugely expensive container rat race, where small, cramped, comfortless ships rush containers from the smaller, shallower ports to feed the mammoth ocean-going boxboats at the main deepwater terminals. Instead, they gracefully withdrew into shipbroking and chartering.

That four out of five of their final ships, all well past their twentieth birthdays, were sold on for further useful seagoing service speaks well not only of the company's ownership and careful husbandry but of the ships and their men themselves. The Golden Liberties were - and some still are - indeed a fitting tribute to their illustrious Liberty ship ancestors.

TWO FUNNEL FINALE?

Although it is unlikely that all two-funnelled cargo liners have been identified, photographs of further ships of this type have been slow to turn up in recent months. John Bartlett brought to our attention a photograph of *Stirling Castle* credited to the Nautical Photo Agency. This print was obtained from the National Maritime Museum, who hold much of the former NPA collection. Investigating her history revealed that she was a remarkable ship.

Builders were John Elder and Company of Govan who launched her on 21st January 1882 for the 'Stirling Castle' Steamship Owners Co. Ltd., managed by Thomas Skinner and Co. of London. It cannot be positively stated that *Stirling Castle* met our criteria for a cargo liner in that she did *not* have accommodation for more than 12 passengers when photographed, as she later operated as a passenger-cargo ship, albeit after one funnel was removed. However, it is likely that she had no room for passengers in her early days, as she carried an extraordinary number of firemen, no fewer than 111 on her second voyage from Hankow to London with tea in 1883, according to David MacGregor's *The China Bird* (Chatto and Windus, London, 1961). On this occasion she came home in a record time of just over 27 days, averaging a very creditable 16½ knots. Intended to beat the tea clippers, such speeds were simply not economical with the compound engines of 1882, and *Stirling Castle* is said to have burned up to 180 tons of coal *a day*. She was sold after her 1883 passage, becoming the *Nord America* of M. Bruzzo e Compagnia of Genoa, who used her to start a service between Italy and South America under the title La Veloce Linea di Navigazione Italiana a Vapore, 'The Rapid Italian Steamship Line.' Bonsor's exhaustively-researched *North Atlantic Seaway* (David and Charles, Newton Abbot, 1975), from which her later career details have mostly been obtained, says that, because of her fame as *Stirling Castle*, she was allowed to carry this name as well as *Nord America*. Her service between Italy and South America was interrupted at least twice by charters to foreign governments for troop carrying. The British used her in 1885, and the Russians in 1899 when she took troops from Odessa to Vladivostok in connection with the Boxer Rebellion in China. In 1901 she was sent to the Tyne where Palmers replaced her compound machinery with triple-expansion engines, in so doing reducing her speed to 13½ knots. Bonsor notes that her funnels were heightened at this time, her mizzen mast removed, and her passenger accommodation modified. He does not say whether this accommodation had been fitted when new, however. *Nord America* then made a number of voyages from Italy to New York with emigrants, and continued until 1909 after which she worked as a pure cargo ship. On 5th December 1910 she stranded on the coast of Morocco whilst bound from Buenos Aires to Genoa with a cargo of horses. Although refloated, she was then laid up at Genoa for three years before being broken up. *[National Maritime Museum P14020]*

The second photograph, kindly loaned by Tony Smith, custodian of the World Ship Photo Library, shows the *Iolani* of Glasgow. Built at Port Glasgow in 1881 for Raeburn and Verel, she appears to have her owner's red funnels with black tops. Again, we have no positive evidence that *Iolani* was *not* built to carry passengers, and indeed she may have conveyed people later in life, but her original

Glasgow owners are strongly associated with pure cargo ships. *Iolani* was sold in 1891, and just a year later was renamed *Crescent*. This name, and her subsequent ownership by Hajee Cassum Mooja of Durban, suggests that she was involved in the pilgrim trade, but evidence is lacking. *Crescent* was broken up at Bombay in February 1903 after a comparatively short life.

Although we usually aim to include photographs of good technical quality, we have made an exception in the case of the third illustration which is probably very rare. It was sent by Robert A. Wettling, of Gahanna, Ohio, who wrote as follows.

'While reading *Record* - as usual, with great interest - the drawing of the Japanese ships, *Hyogo Maru* and *Osaka Maru* (*Record* 9, p. 41) looked very familiar. I recalled the May 1942 issue of *Marine Engineering and Shipping Review* had pictures of modern Japanese ships. While the enclosed copy of the picture is just that - not a photograph - I though it was definitely the same ship. The picture also shows the lattice work in question.'

SOURCES AND ACKNOWLEDGEMENTS

Photographs are from the collection of John Clarkson unless otherwise credited. We thank all who gave permission for their photographs to be used, and for help in finding photographs we are particularly grateful to David Whiteside and Tony Smith of the World Ship Photo Library; to Ian Farquhar, Bill Laxon, Peter Newall, Ivor Rooke, William Schell, George Scott; to David Hodge and Bob Todd of the National Maritime Museum; Dr. David Jenkins of the National Museums and Galleries of Wales; and other museums and institutions listed.

Research sources have included the *Registers* of William Schell and Tony Starke, *Lloyd's Register, Lloyd's Confidential Index, Lloyd's War Losses, Mercantile Navy Lists,* and *Marine News*. Use of the facilities of the World Ship Society's Central Record, the Guildhall Library, the Public Record Office and Lloyd's Register of Shipping are gratefully acknowledged. Particular thanks also to William Schell and John Bartlett for information, to Heather Fenton for editorial and indexing work, and to Marion Clarkson for accountancy services.

The Lamport and Holt Vs.
In addition to sources listed above, the following were consulted:
Bonsor NRP, *South Atlantic Seaway,* David & Charles, Newton Abbot, 1975
Wilson HW, *The Great War 1920*, volumes 6 and 9.
Lloyd's War Losses: The First World War, Lloyd's of London Press, London, 1990.
Daily Telegraph, 13-17th November 1928.

The Shipping World, 1908-1914 and 1919-1921
Lloyd's List and Shipping Gazette, 1905-1928
Lloyd's Weekly Shipping Index 1905-1917
Lloyd's Daily Shipping Index 1932

Pride and Fall - *the Panmure*
A description of the Dundee Clipper Line can be found in Basil Lubbock, *The Last of the Windjammers*, Volume I, Brown, Son & Ferguson, Ltd., Glasgow, 1927, pp.192-5,470.

Hull in the Hundreds
The sources listed above have been widely used in the compilation of this feature, especially the *Registers* of William Schell and Tony Starke. Other sources were:
Burrell, DCE *Scrap and Build*, World Ship Society, Kendal, 1983.
Haws, D *Merchant Fleets* 9, TCL Publications, Burwash, 1986
Jenkins JG and Jenkins D. *Cardiff Shipowners*, National Libraries and Museums of Wales, Cardiff, 1986
Smith-Hughes J. *Sea Breezes* 1964; 34; 376-80
Spaldin BG and Appleyard HS *The West Hartlepool Steam Navigation Company Limited*, World Ship Society, Kendal, 1980.
Thomas PN. *British Ocean Tramps*, Waine Research Publications, Albrighton, 1992

Margaret Rose
Thanks to Richard Robinson, to Alan Hirst and Peter Horsley and Fleetwood Museum.

MARGARET ROSE
James Pottinger

Having contributed model plans to a number of magazines for about twenty years, covering a wide range of vessels from fishing boats to cargo liners and tankers, I was lucky to obtain general arrangement and lines drawings of the steam trawler *Margaret Rose* from her builders prior to their closure.

The *Margaret Rose* was built by Cochrane and Sons Ltd. at Selby as yard number 1100 and was delivered on 12th March 1931 to the Boston Deep Sea Fishing and Ice Co. Ltd. of Fleetwood, but given the Grimsby fishing number of GY 355. Her main particulars are shown in the box.

> **Particulars of the *Margaret Rose***
> O.N. 161009 428g 172n 145.0 x 25.5 x 14.5 feet
> T. 3-cyl by Amos and Smith Ltd., Hull, 99 IHP;
> cylinder diameters 13.75, 23.5, and 39 ins; and
> stroke 27 ins., supplied by steam from one single-
> ended Scotch boiler with three furnaces.
> Fitted with electric light, wireless, direction finder
> and a 'Fathometer' echo sounder.

The origins of the order were somewhat peculiar in that the hull was a copy of a trawler built by another yard. In 1930 Cochrane's yard was run by the brothers Lewis and Sydney and their cousin Donald. Having only one trawler to finish with no orders to follow they approached Basil and Fred Parkes, owners of the Boston Company, pleading for a further order. This request was agreed to provided they built a vessel of similar lines to the *Daily Mail* (386/1930) by Smith's Dock Co. Ltd. at Middlesborough, the first of the company's cruiser-sterned trawlers. However, as these vessels were somewhat advanced for their day Smith's Dock would not supply the hull lines to Cochranes. This was overcome by taking off full-scale templates of

the stern, bow, hull and rudder shapes whilst the trawler was on the slip, Basil Parkes conveying these to the Selby yard on the roof rack of his Sunbeam car. The trawler was launched by skipper Walter Holmes' wife Margaret and named after her and her daughter Rose. Described as one of the 'super trawlers' of her day, she was the largest trawler then operating out of Fleetwood. *Margaret Rose* completed her maiden voyage on Sunday 5th April 1931 under the command of skipper Walter Holmes, landing 3,760 stones, principally of hake.

In search of US hake
Next year she made an exploratory voyage in search of hake off the coast of North America, grounds never fished by British trawlers. Leaving Fleetwood she was seen off by local councillors, carrying 340 tons of coal, 90 tons of ice, two tons of salt and provisions for her 15 strong crew. Ready for departure she resembled a coal tip with coal packed everywhere after the bunkers were filled to the limit. It was said that her scuppers were two inches below the water on her departure. At this stage the local Board of Trade inspector remonstrated and insisted that a large quantity of the coal be bagged and stowed aft to raise her freeboard forward. The accompanying photograph, which was reproduced with a report in the *West Lancashire Evening Gazette*, certainly shows the trawler well down as she leaves Fleetwood. This voyage was instigated by the skipper who had visited the USA with his wife and Fred Parkes to investigate

Daily Mail, the trawler built by Smith's Dock on whose lines the *Margaret Rose* was based. She had a short life, and was wrecked on the Mull of Galloway on 10th May 1931 whilst returning from the fishing grounds to Fleetwood.

progress with electric trawler winches and to explore the viability of supplying hake to British markets.

After various trials and tribulations due to bad weather, shortage of marketable hake and loss of gear on the fishing grounds, she returned to Grimsby where her catch of 800 boxes of prime haddock was sold for such a low price as to leave her skipper £70 pounds in debt in terms of poundage.

Two views of *Margaret Rose* (GY 355), the lower one showing her leaving Fleetwood to explore US fishing grounds in October 1932. *[Fleetwood Museum]*

France and Spain

On 17th August 1933 the trawler was transferred to French registry as the *Marguerite Rose* under the ownership of Société Anonyme des Pêcheries St Pierre, managed by P.H. Ficheux of Boulogne, quickly being transferred to Pêcheries de la Morinie, both companies being reported as associates of her original owners. Skipper Holmes and several others remained with the vessel for some time as part a large crew of 32, and pioneered deep-

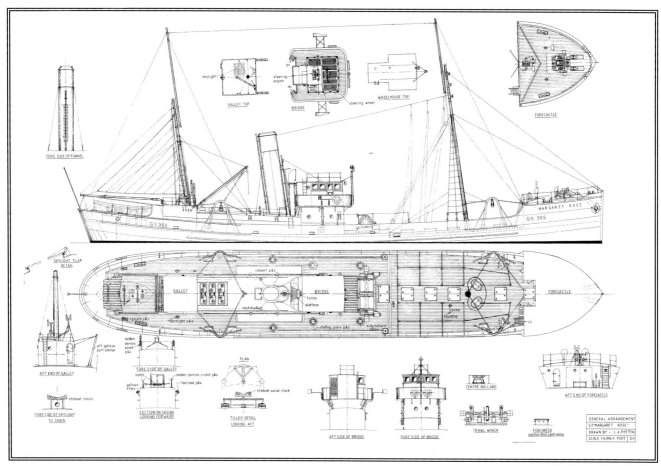

The author's general arrangement drawing of the 1931-built *Margaret Rose* (top).

sea fishing in Norwegian waters from Boulogne. Holmes later returned to the UK to take command of the *Phyllis Rosalie* (433/1934) and after spending over 30 years with the Boston company he bought his own trawler, the *Loch Lein* (111/1948), and took her to New Zealand where he eventually settled.

The saga of the *Margaret Rose* now gets more complicated as there are reports that she was one of three ex-Fleetwood trawlers converted for mercantile use, the Canadian-built *Somersby* (271/1918) and the *Authorpe* (271/1917) being the others, and which worked in the Mediterranean during the Spanish Civil War carrying cargoes between Barcelona, Valencia and Alicante. An item in the *Fleetwood Chronicle* of 18th November 1938 included a report by her second officer Harry Chard that during an air raid on Barcelona the trawler was heavily damaged by bombs, the displacement of water due to the near

The second *Margaret Rose* (GY 716) was actually an older vessel, built at Selby in 1912 (right).
[*World Ship Society Cochrane Collection*]

misses caused the ship to rear up out of the water and her bow then came down on the quayside. Half of the wheelhouse was carried away with damage to the radio room and steering gear casing, and the starboard lifeboat was also damaged. The trawler then went to Marseilles for repairs. The reference to the starboard lifeboat would suggest that additional boats had been fitted since her trawling days.

A cutting from the *Fleetwood Chronicle* of 7th February 1939 included a photo of the trawler claimed to be sunk at the quayside, but I cannot confirm if this was another incident or that referred to above, although the rather indistinct copy could well show her with the bows resting on a quay.

However, Richard Robinson, the WSS Central Record expert on trawlers, points out that Spanish naval records do not list *Marguerite Rose* as being used as a blockade runner, and according to Richard's records she continued fishing out of Bordeaux until August 1939, when she was requisitioned by the French Navy to serve as an auxiliary minesweeper with the pennant number AD 23.

French Warships of World War II claims that she was blown up in the lock pits on 28th May 1940 in an effort to block the dock at Dunkirk. However, other sources suggest that she may have been bombed and sunk off Dunkirk whilst trying to escape to the UK.

A later *Margaret Rose*
From 1936 there was another *Margaret Rose* (348/1912), built by Cook, Welton and Gemmell Ltd. as *Pavlova* (GY 716), and later becoming *Euthamia*. She is listed in Colledge's *Ships of the Royal Navy* as being purchased by the Admiralty as a boom defence vessel in March 1940, and was laid up in 1946. A minor mystery concerns this ship. I have correspondence from a former naval crew member who confirms that he joined the *Margaret Rose* of 348 gross tons in Marseilles on 6th June 1940 to bring her to Greenock, arriving on 17th July 1940. Curiously, he states that the French flag was painted on top of the casing for identification when running the Spanish blockade. If in fact the flag was displayed for this purpose it would be a coincidence if there were two trawlers of almost the same name employed during the Spanish Civil War. After Admiralty service the second *Margaret Rose* was sold in 1946 to owners in Haugesund, Norway and fished as *Morna* until November 1951 when she was broken up at Antwerp.

PUTTING THE RECORD STRAIGHT

Letters, additions, amendments and photographs relating to articles in any issues of *Record* are welcomed. Letters may be lightly edited.

Worcestershire dismasted
I was particularly interested in the two-part article on Bibby's four masters in *Record* 12 and 13, not because of any close affinity with these vessels or their owning company, but because I have always considered the five four-masted ships built between the wars a bit of an anachronism - modern motorships with an outward appearance reflecting an earlier period of merchant ship design. This, of course, was changed in the post-war refits of three of the fleet, following which their lines were more in keeping with merchant design of the period - a great improvement to my mind.

The real subject of this letter is *Worcestershire* and in particular her masts. Your first illustration is of the ship in her pre-war glory with four masts and the second, after the post-war refit, with only one. No mention is made in the text to indicate when she lost her original mainmast, let alone the mizzen and jigger.

After some three years' military service in Burma, I left Rangoon for home in March 1947 on *Worcestershire*. I have a couple of photographs of the ship taken on the day we embarked and both clearly show no second mast. Was this, I wonder, removed during the 1940 conversion to an armed merchant cruiser, during repairs following torpedo damage in 1941, or when she was converted to trooping in 1943? Duncan Haws

makes no mention of masts in his notes on *Worcestershire* in *Merchant Fleets* volume 29. In fact, the removal of the masts does not appear to be accurately documented anywhere as far as any of the ships are concerned, not by *History of the Bibby Line* (1969) and *The Bibby Line 1807-1990* (1990) both published by the company, nor by Duncan Haws. *Record* 13 gives more information on the subject than any other source but even this is incomplete.

A careful study of the *Record* 13 text and illustrations shows that not one of the five ships carried all four masts throughout the conflict. Looking at them, individually, *Shropshire* (as HMS *Salopian*) lost three masts during a 1940 conversion to an armed merchant cruiser which left her with only a foremast. *Cheshire* had the same treatment as evidenced by the 1947 photograph, but the article (and Duncan Haws) omits to tell us when the other three masts were removed. *Staffordshire*, on the other hand, had her fourth (jigger) mast removed sometime during the war as evidenced by the photograph and, in her post-war refit was left with only her foremast.

Worcestershire we know lost her second mast during the war and her mizzen and jigger masts in her post-war refit. Strangely, masts 2, 3 and 4 were not removed when she underwent conversion to an armed merchant cruiser in 1939. Finally, *Derbyshire* was left with only a foremast during conversion to an armed merchant cruiser in 1939 (Duncan Haws confirms this) but regained her mainmast during her post-war refit which gave her a more balanced appearance.

HMT *Worcestershire* in the Rangoon River, 20th March 1947. No official source seems to have kept track of radical changes to a ship's appearance such as the removal of masts. Such data on Bibby's ships has come mainly from observation and photographs, which reinforces the value of always dating photographs. [Ralph Walker, Ray Palmer collection]

All very confusing but interesting nevertheless, and obviously a field for further research.

Another interesting fact is that four of the five motor ships were attacked at some time or the other during the war by torpedo or bombs. It was only *Shropshire* (as HMS *Salopian*) which was lost and that took five torpedo hits - evidence of Fairfield's solid construction.

RAY PALMER, 11 Elm Grove, Southend-on-Sea, Essex SS1 3EY

Red revisions

I write with reference to the *Ilichevsk* featured on page 124 of *Record* 14. As the *Tramore* she was completed for the Black Sea trade with a particular view to the homeward shipment of grain.

It was reported that her Tosi-type four-stroke single-acting air-injection engines gave much trouble at first. The machinery was built under license by Richardson, Westgarth. This concern engined the pioneer motorship launched by Raylton, Dixon and Co. in 1912 for the Furness, Withy group.

The success of *Brazilian Prince*, as *Tramore* became, and her sister *Castilian Prince* ex-*Sycamore* on the New York-River Plate trade led to the commissioning in 1929 of the much larger Compass class cargo passenger liners for this service.

Concerning the British C1-M-AV1 (*Record* 13, pages 54-6), my recollection is that the Vestey Group operated one called *Jutahy* under the Panamanian flag. A friend, a Lamport and Holt man, was one of her mates on the North America to Amazon service in the early 1950s.

ALAN McCLELLAND, 33 Montclair Drive, Mossley Hill, Liverpool L18 0HB.

Jutahy which became Sargent *and another British-owned C1-M-AV1 were missed from our review. They will be featured in a forthcoming issue. Has any reader a photograph of* Jutahy *under this name?*

Three Russian tankers have carried the name *Ural*, the first of which is mentioned in the caption on page 128 as being built in the early 1930s, whilst the third was the diesel-electric tanker dating from 1956. The first *Ural* (7,745/1932) possibly never sailed as such, or was renamed *Josef Stalin* very soon after delivery. Built at the 'Andre Marti' Shipyard, Nikolayev, this twin-screw motor ship had a long history, being renamed *Nikolaev* in 1962, then *Toyo Maru* in 1971. Under the latter name she arrived at Kaohsiung for demolition on 5th December 1971.

Two of the twin screw motorships referred to in Alan McClelland's letter are seen in British ownership. Left is *Brazilian Prince* (3,907/1924), built as *Tramore*, which became *Ilichevsk* as described and illustrated in *Record* 14, page 124. Below is *Sycamore* (3,908/1923) like *Tramore* built for the Johnston Line Ltd. by Furness Shipbuilding Co. Ltd. Renamed *Castilian Prince* in 1915, in 1932 she too was sold to the USSR and had a variety of names: *Enukidze, G. Yagoda,* and *Michurin,* as which she was deleted from *Lloyd's Register* in 1968. She is recorded as carrying the name *Voroshilov* briefly in 1946, although this might be through confusion with her sister. [Upper: F.W. Hawks]

The second *Ural* (6,100/1934), which I think is the tanker illustrated on page 128, emerged from the same yard in 1934 and appeared in *Lloyd's Register* for the last time in 1935. One can only assume that she was requisitioned by the Soviet Navy and retained by them until around 1963. Thereafter, *Ural* (2) appears to have returned to commercial service, and the photograph must have been taken very shortly after the ship's re-appearance. Neither *Lloyd's Register* nor *Marine News* mention this ship in post-war years, but she appeared in the 1964 *Lloyd's Confidential Index* in the USSR fleet list as 'not identified', and the following year is included in the USSR fleet. *Lloyd's Shipping Index* also began to list *Ural* in 1964/65 and continued until 1969, when it is assumed that she was withdrawn from service. During her six years back in commercial service she visited the UK several times, but also traded in the Mediterranean, to Canada and the West Indies.

The third tanker to be named *Ural* was the diesel-electric ship of 1956. She was similar in size to the second *Ural*, and traded in the Mediterranean and to West Africa, with an occasional visit to Newfoundland, presumably to supply fuel to Soviet trawlers. *Ural* (3) was another vessel about which information is sparse. She was not in *Lloyd's Shipping Index* after 1963, nor in the *Confidential Index* after 1970, yet she continued to be listed in *Lloyd's Register* until 1981. *Marine News* is silent on her fate.

I have been unable to establish how *Ural* (1) and (2) were employed during the Second World War. The only Russian tanker I can trace which came under German control was the *Grosni* (4,962/1916) which was captured at Mariupol in October 1941.
JOHN B. HILL, The Hollies, Wall, Hexham, Northumberland NE46 4EQ.
Thanks also to Harold Appleyard and Hubert Hall for information on the mysterious Urals.

I was particularly interested in Richard Pryde's feature 'Vintage Reds', and especially the photograph of the *Professor Popov* (ex-*Flensburg*) one of the six motorships built at Flensburg for the Hugo Stinnes group between 1935 and 1939.

This brought back memories of the four ships of the six which operated the Transocean Transport Line from the U.S. Gulf to Liverpool, Manchester and London during the late 1930s. They were *Clare Hugo Stinnes 1* (1935), *Johannes Molkenbuhr* (1936), *Mathias Stinnes* and *Mulheim Ruhr* (both 1937). All were about 5,330gt.

The other two ships of the group, the *Flensburg* (later *Professor Popov*) and *Welheim* (both 1939) never, as far as I am aware, operated on the Transocean Transport Line, but I regularly saw the other four in Liverpool in 1938-39, just before the outbreak of the war.

I would like to know the fate of the *Welheim*; I wonder can anyone tell me?
CRAIG J.M. CARTER, 15 King's Court, Well Lane, Higher Bebington, Wirral, Merseyside CH63 8QL
According to Gert Detlefsen's Die Stinnes Reedereien, *Welheim was in Port Aransas, Texas on her maiden voyage when war broke out, but returned to Germany disguised as the Norwegian* Mim. *Her end came on 28th November 1944 when sunk by a British motor torpedo boat on a voyage from Bergen to Aalesund.*

Drifter details
It was with interest that I read Stephen Daniel's interpretation of the design and longevity of the steam drifters in *Record* 12. However, I would like to point out the following.

On page 236 the caption for the *Golden News* LT 373 states she is a well-proportioned drifter with a beautiful sheer line, this may be so but she was not built at John Chambers yard in 1914 but by Colby Brothers.

The unidentified English steam drifter on page 238 is the *Silver Seas* LT 235 and was more than likely sailing out of Lowestoft, and not over the bar at Gorleston. A product of Cochrane and Son of Selby in 1931, her triple-expansion engine built by Elliott and Garrood of Beccles was removed in 1960 and replaced by a three-cylinder 4SA 300 BHP engine by AK Diesel Ltd. of Lowestoft, the conversion to motor being carried out by

LBS Engineering of Lowestoft. She was re-registered as *Silver Seas* A 65 and broken up in 1971.

The classic MFV cruiser stern is now disappearing in Scotland although several skippers are reconsidering the design due to reverting back to seine netting to get away from the heavy fuel costs of various types of trawling.

The print of the *Alpha* YH 421 on page 241 showing her fallen on her side on the ways is on the grid at North Shields. As is stated, some discussion as to which was the first purpose-built steam drifter has taken place, but the *Alpha* was two years later than the two which I believe to be the first. *Onward* LH 880 was built 1877 by D. Allan of Granton with a compound steam engine by J.O. Spence of North Shields and built for the Forth Steam Fishing Co. of Leith. She was sold to France in 1897. *Forward* KY 505 was also built in 1877 by D. Allan with a compound steam engine by J.O. Spence of North Shields and built for Sharp and Murray of Cellardyke. She was lost in the North Sea during 1890.

The details given for the *Alpha* are confusing because she was built by J. McKenzie of Thurso in 1879 with a 14" stroke compound steam engine. Registered at Great Yarmouth in 1899 she was sold in 1908 to the Devon Brick and Tile Co of Exmouth and is believed to have been converted to a steam coaster for her new owners. Her loss details seem to be erroneous as the only Three Kings Rocks I know are at Cullen. A steam drifter was actually named after these rocks, the *Three Kings* BF 495, which later found her way to Lowestoft as LT 517.

Stephen Daniels goes on to say that the *Lydia Eva* was the only steam drifter built at Kings Lynn. The yard of Crichton Thompson at Kings Lynn built two standard steam drifters for the Admiralty in 1921. *Melody*, Admiralty number 4172, was delivered on 4th February 1921, renamed *Rose Duncan* and ended her life at Lowestoft as *Lord Duncan* LT 273, sailing for the breakers in October 1954. *Morn*, Admiralty number 4173 was delivered 17th March 1921 and was renamed *Homefinder, Bene Vertat*, and *Defensor*.

This yard became the Kings Lynn Shipbuilding Co. Ltd. and then the Kings Lynn Slipway Co. Ltd., which built the *Lydia Eva* YH 89. Although the *Lydia Eva* had somewhat unusual lines for a steam drifter with a pronounced bluff bow these lines were very similar to those of the two ships built at this yard in 1929 for Spanish pair fishing, the *Angel C.* and the *Rosario C.* of similar tonnage but slightly shorter than the *Lydia Eva*.

Incidentally, the two ships were taken to San Sebastian by Yarmouth crews which then brought back to Lowestoft the Spanish-registered *Ni Tu*, formerly the Yarmouth steam drifter *Homocea* YH 214, which on arrival at Lowestoft became *Homocea* LT 112. She was converted to motor in 1953 and renamed *Strenuous* LT 112, being broken up in 1964. She was built as HM Drifter *Waterfall* by A. Hall and Co. at Aberdeen in 1919.

The account by Fred Kilgour of sailing out of Fleetwood in 1950 on a fishing trip in the *Rose Hilda* YH 73 (*Record* 13) was very interesting. The *Rose Hilda* was built on spec by Fellows and Co. of Great Yarmouth in 1929 and was completed in 1930. She was offered to prospective owners but turned down as she was not a motor ship. She was sold to W.J.E. Green Ltd. and registered on 26th March 1930 as *Rose Hilda* YH 73. Prior to her sale to 'Wee Green' as he was known, he had a disagreement with his brother over the engine which was of the triple-expansion type built by F. W. Carver whose premises stood on the south side of the south dry dock in Fellows' yard and still stands today, although the south dry dock has been filled in. The *Rose Hilda* was rebuilt as a motor ship in 1954 and renamed *Dawn Waters* LT 90 and broken up in 1970.

The *Romany Rose* YH 63 was built by John Chambers of Lowestoft and, although she did win the Prunier Trophy under skipper Walter Rudd, she was not a sister ship to the *Rose Hilda*. This was the *Vigia* also built on spec as a drifter/trawler and which lay on the stocks for several years before being finished in 1936 as a motor pilot cutter/Trinity House tender named *Vigia*. She was later lost in the North Sea in her new role as a survey vessel to the oil industry.

Keep the good work up on this excellent quality publication.
BARRY BANHAM, 240 Lowestoft Road, Gorleston, Great Yarmouth, Norfolk NR31 WQ

Troublesome Swans and more on tankers

It is appropriate that *Toiler* and *Tynemount* share page 249 of *Record* 12, as they both warrant places in the records. Classed by the British Corporation they were sisters, the surveyor noting *Tynemount* had 'scantlings similar to *Toiler*.'

Toiler had two Swedish-built medium speed (250 rpm) four-cylinder, two-stroke Polar diesels driving twin screws. The surveyor noted 160 BHP each, others give 180 BHP. The British Corporation survey book states that she was completed April 1911, likely reflecting her machinery: the engine surveyor visited her up to 2nd May 1911.

For a novel ship she led a remarkable life, being twice re-engined and converted to a single screw steamer. In 1914 she was fitted with a compound built by Detroit Engine Works in 1889. In 1929 she was given a Polson Iron Works triple-expansion engine dating from 1903. From whence came these engines?

Tynemount's hull was subcontracted to Smith's Dock (No. 541) by Swan Hunter and Wigham Richardson (No. 908) who then completed her. The British Corporation surveyor initially gave Montreal Transportation Co. Ltd. as owners, then changed this to the Electric Marine Propulsion Co. Ltd. This may hint at her intended ownership.

The Electric Marine Propulsion Co. Ltd. was owned by Mavor and Coulson Ltd, the Glasgow electrical engineers. It was formed in April 1912 to acquire Mavor's patents, and of the £39,000 capital issued over £35,000 was with Mavor interests. Swan Hunter had a nominal £1,000. On the failure of *Tynemount* Electric Marine Propulsion Co. Ltd. was placed in liquidation during February 1914.

Launched on 26th March 1913, *Tynemouth* ran trials on 17th September. A pair of Mirrlees four-stroke, six-cylinder diesels ran at 400 rpm coupled to Mavor and Coulson alternators powering an AC electric motor on a single screw. The electrical installation was a failure. She was re-engined and sold in September 1914 to Reuben McLelland of Kingston, Ontario. Mirrlees took the diesels back and I believe they were re-used. She now had a triple-expansion engine from Earles of Hull and went on trials as a steamer on 9th July 1914.

Since I wrote my two funnel tanker article (*Record* 13), Bill Schell has suggested the two Cleveland built ships, *Minnetonka* and *Minnewaska*, were intended for ocean, as opposed to Great Lakes, service. This has been confirmed by reported movements in *Lloyd's Weekly Shipping Index*. They came down to Quebec in two sections. The *Shipping Index* reported *Minnewaska* as being joined together and coming out of dry dock at Quebec on 21st October 1902. *Minnetonka* preceded her sister. They were renamed *Santa Maria* and *Santa Rita* at Newport News. The Shipping Index reported them sailing for San Francisco under their new names on 28th May 1906.

It may be a little too late to refer back to *Record 8* (no! ed), but I was able to look at the First Survey for the Atlantic, one of the four ships the subject of John Hill's article 'The Tanker That Never Was.' The list of dates that I have compiled so far is as follows:

Y/N	Name	Keel	Launch	Trials
978	*Scottish Strath*	20.10.20	29.12.21	11.7.22
979	*Scottish Castle*			
981	*Scottish Highlands/ Lubrafol*		16.7.24	
982	*Scottish Monarch/ Atlantic*	5.12.21	24.3.25	8.8.25

Although not complete the keel-laying date for *Atlantic* would tend to confirm the identity of 981/982 as being the two missing orders for Tankers Ltd.

DAVID BURRELL, 63, Avisyard Avenue, Cumnock, Ayrshire KA18 MJ

Pontoon demise postponed

I write regarding the letter 'Off and on the Canal' from Ken Lowe in *Record* 13, referring to the photograph on page 219 in *Record* 12.

I think that the pontoon may have survived beyond the mid 1960s. I photographed the pontoon of Manchester Dry Docks Ltd., Ship Engine and Boiler Repairers, just above Mode Wheel Lock on the 9th August 1975. At that time it had the *Otterspool* of Liverpool moored alongside. The pontoon appeared to be the same one, but the walkways along both sides had much more substantial supports.

DEREK ATHERTON, 3 Twyford Place, Fingerpost, St. Helens, Merseyside WA9 1BN

Swansea tug identity

In *Ships in Focus Blue Funnel Line* page 56 shows a tug lying astern of *Eurydamas* at Swansea. The date is between 1915 and 1924. Funnel colours are black with two white bands, the same as BI or United (Ring) Tugs of Gravesend, and upperworks are dark with a white band round the hull. I can make out that the name has four letters ending in A. My research eliminates a BI or Ring tug. Can anyone tell me the name and owner of this vessel?

J W GRAINGER, Kyrenia, Second Avenue, Hook End, Brentwood, Essex CM15 OHH

John B. Hill has sent this photograph of the *Smok* which allows us to complete the illustration of all the Polskarob vessels listed in *Record* 13. Completed as the coal bunkering vessel *Robur VII*, after capture by the Germans in 1939 she was converted to a salvage vessel, returning via USSR ownership to Poland in 1947, where she became *Smok*. After undertaking some notable salvage operations, including the battle cruiser *Gneisenau*, she survived until 1990. She was then taken to Spain to be scrapped - quite a journey for what had been built as a harbour craft.

Port Line postcripts

Although not illustrated in the Port Line feature in *Record* 13, the *Port Adelaide* was one of the better looking ships which bridged the transition from the more upright design of older vessels to the more extreme 'streamlining', although never excessive, of later designs.

Some time ago I was drawing up model plans of this ship based on the general arrangement drawings and photographs published in the *Motor Ship* at the time of her maiden voyage, aided by some photos of the ship I took on the Clyde. It was only when well into the project that I noted that the views did not agree; in fact, the later photographs show the ship with two unevenly-spaced sets of goalpost masts on the fore deck, whereas she was originally fitted with a single raking pole mast between hatches no.2 and 3. The later vertical goal post masts were quite narrowly spaced, mounted just out board of existing mast house, as my photo below shows.

Perhaps some reader could tell us when this alteration was carried out.

JAMES A. POTTINGER, 1 Jesmond Circle, Bridge-of-Don, Aberdeen AB22 8WX

I've just finished reading *Record* 13 and, as usual, thoroughly enjoyed it.

Just a very few comments which may be of use.

Page 24: *Lucigen*. The date of her scuttling was 5th July 1946.

Page 26: Port Line's Golden Era. It was sad that a photo of the *Port Brisbane*, the very first of the streamliners, was not included. *Port Launceston* and *Port Invercargill* were both built at Belfast. Only the *Port Montreal* was built at Govan.

BILL LAXON, Waimarana, Upper Whangateau Road, PO Box 171, Matakana 1240, New Zealand.

Missing from the Port Line feature in *Record* 13 was the Swan, Hunter-built *Port Brisbane* (11,942/1949). After 26 years in Port Line ownership, she arrived at Hong Kong to be broken up in November 1975.

It was interesting to see the variations of funnel markings in Peter Newall's article 'Port Line's Golden Era' (*Record* 13 page 26). Both *Port Townsville* and *Port Melbourne*, pictured in Adelaide, are in the colours of the Compass Line, a service started by Blue Star Line and Port Line in 1969 between South Africa and Australia. The funnel had a black top with a blue base with a thin white line dissecting the two. On the blue was a white circle containing a red compass point design. *Port Melbourne* took the first sailing in October 1969 but poor results saw the company's withdrawal in March 1971.

The fine J.Y. Freeman photograph of *Port St Lawrence* in Sydney on page 26 shows the vessel with an Atlas Line funnel - a similar design to Compass Line but with a red strip through the middle of the white circle. The short-lived service of the Atlas Line was an attempt by the Australian partners of Associated Container Transportation Ltd. (ACT) - Blue Star Line, Port Line and Ellermans - to gain a share of the Australia-Japan trade. They had applied to the conference for a trade share but were rebuffed. *Rockhampton Star* took the first sailing in September 1967 but after a short freight war lasting two months, the British interests in the Australian Eastern Conference, led by P & O and Ocean, came to an agreement with the three errant lines that whenever a container service was developed from Australia to Japan, the Atlas Line members would be able to obtain a minority interest from the existing British Lines' trade share. This option was

James Pottinger's photograph of the Hawthorn, Leslie-built *Port Adelaide* (8,106/1951) in the Clyde. Her career was briefer than that of *Port Brisbane*, and she arrived at Kaohsiung to be broken up in August 1972.

never exercised as in a later deal in April 1971, P & O interests, through the New Zealand Shipping Company, agreed to withdraw from the East Coast North America-Australia and New Zealand container service, subject to the other three carriers in the trade (Blue Star Line, Port Line and Ellermans) not exercising the rights they had obtained from the Atlas Line foray into the Japanese trade in 1967.

Port Launceston, shown in Wellington on page 28, has a red and white Hamburg-Sud funnel while the vessel was on a time-charter to that company for an outward voyage from Europe to New Zealand on the New Zealand European Shipping Association conference berth in the second half of 1970.

IAN FARQUHAR, RD2, Dunedin, New Zealand

Torquay points

As an expatriate Devonian, the article on Torquay Harbour in *Record* 13 was of particular interest to me. The transom of the *Emily* in the photograph on page 30 is of interest for two reasons. Firstly, it quotes both the home port and the port of registry. Secondly, a feature unique to my mind is her owner's monogram.

Lloyd's List dated 18th April 1881 records her fate: 13.4.1881: *Emily* of Tynemouth (sic), West Hartlepool for Torquay, coal (Captain H. Duckham) in collision 14 miles north east of Whitby with the steamer *Wear* (776/1865) of Sunderland and foundered. Crew saved. Richard and Bridget Larn, in their *Wrecks of the British Isles*, Volume 3, section CE agree with the date and location, but quote an improbable voyage of Runcorn to Jersey.

Turning to the photograph on page 31, the vessel with painted ports is a schooner with a standing gaff and brailed foresail on the foremast. This and other features of her rigging rule out her being *Emily*. Her port of registry appears to be ___*mouth*.

Incidentally, the *Lady Sophia* (page 35) was sunk in 1969 not 1979.

Keep up the good work - particularly with the likes of the Bristol (*Record* 12) and Torquay photographs.

MARTIN BENN, 5 Grove Road, Walton-le-Dale, Preston PR5 4AJ.

Martin also confirms John Naylon's identification in Record *14, page 110 of* Johannes *as the vessel built at Ronne in 1902.*

As a retired motor barge skipper I was very interested to read the report on Torquay Harbour (part 2) in the 1930s (*Record* 14).

However, I must dissent from the remarks on page 106 that *Goldeve* was one of a class of five ships, the actual number was four as the *Goldace*, the first of the five vessels built for Goldsmith by J. Pollock at Faversham in 1931/1932, was a very different and superior vessel to the following four, *Goldbell*, *Goldcrown*, *Goldrift* and *Goldeve*.

The *Goldace* was a little single-screw motor coaster with dimensions 99 x 21.6 x 7.6 feet and gross tonnage of 158 and a deadweight capacity of about 200 tons. She was a standard design of Pollocks and almost an exact copy of the successful *Ferrocrete* built in 1927 for Blue Circle Cement.

The *Goldbell* class were a modification of the older Goldsmith Dutch-built sailing barges built 1903/04 which were also converted to motor barges by Pollock in the early 1930s, both classes being twin screw. The difference in the two above types is shown below with the *Gothic* representing the Dutch-built vessels.

Type	Dimensions (feet)	Gross tons	Cargo to sea(tons)
Gothic	90.3 x 23.0 x 9.0	156	240
Goldbell	94.5 x 22.8 x 8.8	178	260

From the above it is evident that the newer vessels were slightly longer and of less beam and I wondered if these were any improvement in terms of steering on the Gothic type, known by all who worked aboard them as 'dreadful'. To this end I inquired from Bob Wells, a retired master of both sailing and motor barges (who is now well into his eighties) and who in his youthful days

had sailed in the *Goldeve* as mate - but not for long! His reply to my query - and I quote his words - was that they were 'absolute bastards' to steer when fully laden. The standard of accommodation in the Gothic-class can only be described as 'poor' and no attempt had been made to provide any form of insulation and condensation remained a problem in all of Goldsmith's steel barges.

I well remember my first trip in the Gothic-class *Kentish Hoy* (2), ex-*Maymon* ex-*Teutonic* which was from London to Ipswich with 225 tons of wheat. The weather was fine and clear but a fresh north east wind was kicking up a lively sea on the ebb. Although it was chilly in the wheelhouse I found that I needed no jacket on when steering. Upon docking at Ipswich I saw coming along the quay a well-known coasting barge master by the name of Frank Ellis who stopped and asked how I was getting on with steering the *Kentish Hoy*. I replied that I could not properly steer a compass course in daylight let alone in darkness. He replied that the man who could steer a course with that 'cow' had yet to be born. And how he had done his first and last trip in the *Kentish Hoy* from London to Middlesbrough with scrap iron and telephoned the owners with his resignation adding he would return home by train. In due course the writer was thrown over the wheel when trying to light a cigarette and when half stunned I stood up and found that my vessel had turned herself round and was waddling back towards Sheerness.

Late in 1954 the *Kentish Hoy* began to leak badly whilst loading cement at Halling and, failing to secure a reasonable estimate for repair, was sold to BISCO for scrapping. So, at 2 am on the snowy morning of 12th February 1955 I delivered *Kentish Hoy* at the end of a towrope to T.W. Ward Ltd. at Columbia Wharf, Grays. What grieved me was that on board was about 700 gallons of diesel which the shipbreakers would not pay for. The following morning I received a receipt for the vessel, which document measured 6 x 5 inches.

BOB CHILDS, 45 St. Margarets Street, Rochester, Kent ME11 UF

The builder of *Roselyne* in Gouda, Holland, must be H. van Vlaardingen, this being the only yard there building this type of vessels at that time (*Record 13*). She is an interesting vessel and needs further research as nothing is known about her history or late names before 1928.

No, *Lloyd's Register* did not lose trace of *Reina II*. She is duly mentioned as *Antonina Barraco* from 1967 to 1976, when owned by Giuseppe Barraco of Trapani. She is deleted in 1977 and not mentioned in the casualty returns for 1976 or 1977. According to the *Registro Italiano Navali*, however, she was broken up in 1976.

The *Pax I* (page 104) was bought in November 1942 by the Nazi shipping company Nederlandsche Oost-Reederij NV, Rotterdam but in spite of this she was requisitioned by the Kriegsmarine at the end of 1944 and put under the German flag. After the capitulation of Germany she was taken over by the Dutch Government and was sold by them in October 1950 to Mello Wedema who renamed her *Lyra*. Her end came earlier than stated: she was sold in January 1973 to Frank Rijsdijk Holland NV at Hendrik-Ido-Ambacht for breaking up after a long period of lay up at Harlingen. I have seen the *Stella Maris* there several times, completely worn out.

Drittura was indeed sold in January 1994 and rebuilt as an auxiliary recreation sailing vessel, and is now named *Store Boelt*.

MARTIN LINDENBORN, Postbus 5125, NL-6802 EC, Arnhem, Netherlands

Olympic not Titanic?

Referring to *Burns and Laird* page 28 and the follow-up in *Record* 13 page 58, the ship in the fitting-out basin in Belfast is, in my opinion, the *Olympic* and not the *Titanic*. The *Titanic* had the promenade deck enclosed when she was built and was painted black. The *Olympic* when launched was pale grey and was painted black months later.

NORMAN LEATHERBARROW, 7 Newborough Avenue, Great Crosby, Lancashire L23 9TU.

The top photograph shows *Goldace*, almost certainly just after she had been launched at Faversham: note Goldsmith's blue, white and red pennant at the foremast. Her original Bolinder engine was replaced in 1947 by a twin-cylinder Crossley, and soon afterwards Goldsmiths sold her to T.G. Irving Ltd. of Sunderland who renamed her *Ashdene*. The little motor coaster went for breaking up in 1969.

The sailing barge lines of *Goldcrown* are evident in the second photograph, as is the unusual practice of painting the owner's name on the stern. *Goldcrown* was not a particularly fortunate ship, as she was wrecked near Duncansby Head in the Pentland Firth on 21st September 1942 whilst being towed from Scapa Flow to Buckie by the tug *St. Olaves* (468/1919) which was also wrecked. [Both: Bob Childs collection]

Along with a good crop of letters, David Eeles' feature on Torquay in *Records* 13 and 14 inspired Terry Nelder to send this postcard (bottom) showing the 554-ton steamer *John Johnasson* 'foundered' alongside Torquay's South Pier on 10th October 1907. The steamer was something of a veteran, having been built by Charles Mitchell and Co. at Low Walker in 1870 for a J. Johnasson, then resident in London. Her first voyage was from Newcastle to London, and it is likely she spent much of her life in the coal trade, coastwise and across to the Baltic. Subsequent owners in Sunderland and West Hartlepool did not bother to change her name, and at the time of her accident in Torquay *John Johnasson* was owned by a Hans B. Olsen. Despite his name, Olsen was domiciled in West Hartlepool, which was renowned for giving a home to shipowners and others from elsewhere in Europe, helping to give rise to jokes about 'British West Hartlepool'.

HULL IN THE HUNDREDS

With the year 2001 here, and the new century, *Record* looks back to the first decade of the twentieth century, the 'hundreds' for want of a better name. From the building and loss or sale dates of the ships depicted, these photographs were taken by Marcus Barnard of Hull around one hundred years ago. Most show tramp steamers, many of which never survived the First World War. In many cases Barnard's photographs may well be the only images left to us of these vessels. The ships are described in the somewhat arbitrary order of their owners' base, working clockwise from Hull.

FLAWYL (above)
Sunderland Shipbuilding Co. Ltd., Sunderland; 1906, 3,592gt, 346 feet
T. 3-cyl. by the North Eastern Marine Engineering Co. Ltd., Sunderland.
Not surprisingly, Hull's small band of tramp ship owners are well represented amongst Barnard's photographs. *Flawyl* was owned by the Amyl Steamship Co. Ltd., and managed by William Tulley and Co., who began business in 1873. Her funnel is black with generous red over white bands. The company did not survive the loss of the *Flawyl*, which was torpedoed on 2nd May 1918 by *UB 52*, thirty miles east south east of Pantellaria whilst on a voyage from Malta to Bizerta with a cargo described simply as 'metals'.

QUEENBOROUGH (opposite top)
William Gray and Co. Ltd., West Hartlepool; 1903, 2,961gt, 325 feet
T. 3-cyl. by Central Marine Engine Works, West Hartlepool.
Another modest Hull shipowner, G.R. Sanderson and Co., is represented by the long-bridge deck tramp *Queenborough*, her owning company being less modestly titled the Hull Steam Shipping Co. Ltd. Sanderson was previously in partnership as Moran and Sanderson, but was in business on his own from 1891. He had

four steamers in 1907, but sold out in 1910 when *Queenborough* passed, without change of name, to Hopkins, Jones and Co. She was not to remain long with these Cardiff owners, and 1914 saw her sold to A.M. Coulouthros of Andros in Greece to become *Taigetos*. Her Greek neutrality did not save her from German submarines, and on 24th June 1917 she was torpedoed by *UC 65* in the Bay of Biscay.

GRAPHIC (opposite middle)
William Gray and Co. Ltd., West Hartlepool; 1895, 2,490gt, 304 feet
T. 3-cyl. by Central Marine Engine Works, West Hartlepool.
Easily the longest-lived of the Hull tramp owners was W.H. Cockerline and Co., buying their first steamer in 1885 and surviving until 1954. *Graphic* displays their black funnel with very broad red band and their red-and-white-striped houseflag which was in the distinctive shape of a truncated pennant. Her timber deck cargo was typical of Cockerline's ships, which traded mainly to the Baltic.

This photograph may have been taken earlier than the others in this feature, as *Graphic* was only with Cockerlines from 1895 to 1901. In the latter year she was sold to the first of a series of Greek owners, C. A. Tsiropinas of Syra.

The name he bestowed on her, *Emmanuel*, served throughout her career under the Greek flag. On 4th January 1925 she stranded near St. David's Head whilst bound from Manchester to Bordeaux in ballast. Salvage took several months, and when *Emmanuel* was refloated on 24th March she was fit only for scrap. T.W. Ward Ltd. began demolishing her in Milford Haven in May 1925.

AGNES (opposite bottom)
S.P. Austin and Son Ltd., Sunderland; 1900, 2,845gt, 323 feet
T. 3-cyl. by the North Eastern Marine Engineering Co. Ltd., Newcastle-on-Tyne.
This photograph was taken between 1900 and 1913, when *Agnes* was owned by Lambert Brothers of London: note their houseflag being raised or lowered at the main. AGNES was sold to Spain in 1913, and continued ownership in Bilbao and Valencia may have spared her from predators during both World Wars, although she got caught up in the ferocities of the Spanish Civil War. It would be tiresome to recite her changes of ownership, but she carried the names *Asuarca*, *Almiral Luis de Requesens* and - from 1924 - *Rita Sister*. Under the last of these names she was broken up in Spain early in 1961: by then a very elderly lady indeed.

CLUDEN (above)
*John Readhead and Sons, South Shields;
1896, 3,166gt, 315 feet
T. 3-cyl. by John Readhead and Sons,
South Shields.*

When Jack Smith-Hughes published a series of fleet lists in *Sea Breezes* in the 1960s, he used the running title 'Forgotten Fleets'. Now, a third of a century on, many more fleets - indeed a large proportion of the British tramp industry - could merit the title. And there will be virtually no-one who has been alive long enough to have known and forgotten companies which he featured - including Steel, Young and Co., owners of *Cluden*.

According to Smith-Hughes, a G. Steel of West Hartlepool had his first ship

built in 1873, the 972gt *Solway*, and a year later transferred it to Steel, Young and Company, which established its offices in London. Expansion was rapid if fitful, with periods of fast growth followed by periods of consolidation. Names were varied, with other river names such as *Nith* (1,156/1874) and *Wandle* (1,783/1883) being used alongside place names such as *Wiltshire* (534/1876) and *Roehampton* (2,155/1882).

Cluden was a rather basic flush-decker, and her colour scheme was, to say the least, distinctive for the period. She appears to have had a grey lower hull with the upper strakes of her hull painted black. A photograph of *Chevington* (3,876/1912) accompanying Smith-Hughes' article confirms that *Cluden* was not alone in

having this livery. Funnel colours were less unusual: red with a very broad white band and black top: the red base not being visible in the photograph of *Cluden*.

Cluden was to become a war loss, torpedoed by *U 39* off the coast of Algeria on 22nd October 1916, whilst bringing a cargo of wheat from Karachi to Cardiff. As with so many of the companies whose ships are portrayed in this feature, Smith, Young and Company did not long survive the ravages of the First World War. No ships were added to the fleet after 1912, although the *War Manor* (3,106/1918) was managed briefly for the British Government. In 1919, the surviving ships were sold and Smith, Young and Company was quietly forgotten about.

FENAY LODGE (opposite bottom)
*J. L. Thompson and Sons Ltd., Sunderland;
1904, 3,223gt, 326 feet
T. 3-cyl. by J. Dickinson and Sons Ltd.,
Sunderland.*
The word 'forgotten' seems inappropriate
for Charles Cockroft, the owner of *Fenay
Lodge*, who can hardly have been
described as prominent even in his heyday.
Fenay Bridge (3,838/1910) was the only
other ship owned by his London-based
Fenay Steam Ship Company Ltd.

Fenay Lodge was a neat three-
island steamer with a composite
superstructure which makes her look
smaller than her contemporaries in this
feature, although in fact she was very much
a standard sized tramp of the period. Also
typical was her fate. On 6th March 1917 she
was torpedoed and sunk by *U 44* 250 miles
off Fastnet whilst carrying a cargo of pit
props from Mobile to Cherbourg. With
Fenay Bridge having been torpedoed and
sunk in the Atlantic in March 1916,
Cockcroft was now without ships.

ALDGATE (above)
*Richardson, Duck and Co., Stockton-on-
Tees; 1892, 3,380gt, 340 feet
T. 3-cyl. by G. Blair and Co. Ltd., Stockton-
on-Tees.*
During her British career *Aldgate* had
three owners, but only one manager, H.W.
Dillon of London. Dillon initially registered
her under the Aldgate Steamship Co. Ltd.,
moving her in 1898 to the London Gate
Steamship Co. Ltd., and in 1903 to the
Dowgate Steamship Co. Ltd., a company
he had set up when he began owning
steamers in 1888.

Aldgate has a particularly full
outfit of derricks for a tramp, and the gaff
on the foremast instead of the mainmast is
an unusual feature. She was sold in 1910,
and passed through the hands of four
Genoese owners, who gave her the names
Elio, D'Aosta, and *Indipendente*. She was
broken up in 1928.

CARPATHIAN (below)
*Armstrong, Whitworth and Co. Ltd.,
Newcastle-on-Tyne; 1908, 4,900gt, 385 feet
T. 3-cyl. by the Wallsend Slipway Co. Ltd.,
Newcastle-on-Tyne.*
It is not immediately apparent that
Carpathian is a tanker - she has a good set
of derricks - and only a light catwalk
across her holds gives the game away.
Owners were the Petroleum Steamship Co.
Ltd., and management by Lane and
Macandrew of London is indicated by the
black-topped white funnel with its black
rings. In 1918 managers became the
British Tanker Co. Ltd. and she was
renamed *British Peer*, transferring to the
ownership of this company in 1921. From
1930 she ran for Italian owners as *Tampico*,
and survived the depredations of British
submarines only to fall into German hands
in September 1943. The cause of her
subsequent sinking at Venice is unclear.
After the war *Tampico* was raised and
broken up.

EDALE (above)
R. Craggs and Sons, Middlesbrough; 1901, 3,110gt, 325 feet
T. 3-cyl. by Richardsons, Westgarth and Co. Ltd., Hartlepool.
Bristol is not a port much associated with tramp ships, and standard texts list just two owners of such vessels. Lucas and Company were comparative latecomers to steam, owning nothing but sail until 1893. They then established a modest fleet of tramps, mostly with names taken from north country valleys remote from Bristol, in the ownership of the Dale Steamship Co. Ltd. A letter D for Dale is just discernable on *Edale's* funnel: records suggest that this was red on a yellow basic funnel. As if to reinforce her northern connections, *Edale* carried the name Middlesbrough on her stern, as did other Dale ships (see *Milldale* ex-*Morpeth* below), suggesting Lucas was an exile from Tees-side.

Edale was a relatively early war loss. On 1st May 1915 she was torpedoed by *U 30* 45 miles north west by west of the Scilly Isles, homeward bound with a cargo of Argentinian wheat and linseed for Manchester. Lucas and Company were yet another owner to give up the struggle during the First World War, leaving Mark Whitwill as Bristol's only significant tramp owner.

EXMOUTH (below)
Richardson, Duck and Co., Stockton-on-Tees; 1899, 3,923gt, 340 feet
T. 3-cyl. by Blair and Co. Ltd., Stockton-on-Tees.
The booming town of Cardiff was a magnet for ambitious young men in the latter half of the nineteenth century, attracting a number from the West Country who made their mark in shipowning. The Anning family from Appledore were amongst the

first to set up shop across the Bristol Channel, operating sailing ships initially and moving into steam in 1876. A splendid booklet from the National Museum of Wales, *Cardiff Shipowners*, points out that the significance of Annings to Cardiff shipowning exceeded their own modest fleet, in that Henry Radcliffe, W.J. Tatem and William Reardon Smith all served the company early in their careers.

Exmouth was built for a single-ship company, the Exmouth Steamship Co. Ltd., managed by Anning Brothers. She survived the First World War and in 1924 was sold to a company managed by Angelo Scinicariello of Naples, who renamed her *Nimbo*. The depressed trading conditions of the late twenties probably shortened her life, as in December 1929 *Nimbo* returned to the United Kingdom where T.W. Ward Ltd. broke her up.

DARTMOUTH (above)
Richardson, Duck and Co., Stockton-on-Tees; 1903, 3,322gt, 325 feet
T. 3-cyl. by Blair and Co. Ltd., Stockton-on-Tees.
Built four years after the *Exmouth*, the *Dartmouth* is clearly to the same long-bridge deck design, but a little shorter. In this view she displays Anning's simple but distinctive funnel: black with red band bearing a white letter A, and the matching houseflag.

Dartmouth was sold in 1915 to J.C. Gould and Co. of Cardiff, who was allowed to rename her *Greldon*. She was one of the first acquisitions of what was to become a substantial if short-lived shipping empire. Gould's Steamships and Industrials Ltd. comprised both shipowning and shipbuilding companies, the latter

including the builders of *Greldon's* hull and engines. The group was to collapse spectacularly in 1925. However, *Greldon* was not to live to see this. The tramp was lost with all 28 hands when torpedoed by *U 96* near to the North Arklow Light Vessel, not long after leaving Birkenhead with coal for Italy on 8th October 1917.

ASSYRIA (below)
D. and W. Henderson and Co., Glasgow; 1900, 6,354gt, 451 feet
T. 3-cyl. by D. and W. Henderson and Co., Glasgow.
Unlike most of the other ships in this feature, *Assyria* is a cargo liner rather than a tramp. She is included for two reasons. Firstly, no other photograph is known of here, not even Duncan Haws having found a reference to make a drawing in his

Merchant Fleets 9. Secondly, a minor mystery surrounds her: what was a vessel owned by Anchor Line (note their houseflag at the main) doing in Hull? Although the company once had services across the North Sea, these had long been abandoned by the time *Assyria* was delivered in favour of transAtlantic and Indian services from Glasgow and West Coast ports.

Second of the name for Anchor Line, *Assyria* was sold to T. and J. Brocklebank of Liverpool in July 1912, continuing to run to India without change of name. She was sunk on 26th August 1917 when *UB 61* torpedoed her 35 miles northwest of Lough Swilly whilst on a voyage from Glasgow to New York with general cargo.

ASIATIC PRINCE (opposite)

Short Brothers, Sunderland; 1888, 2,183gt, 292 feet

T. 3-cyl. by J. Dickinson, Sunderland.

The oldest vessel pictured here, *Asiatic Prince* was more cargo liner than tramp, but when she was built the distinction was undoubtedly one of employment rather than design features.

She gave original owner John Knott of Newcastle-on-Tyne 20 years' service, and - after passing through the ownership of Prince Line Ltd. - was sold to Greek owners in 1908 to become *Massalia*. Like no fewer than nine of the 15 ships in this feature, she was lost to a German submarine during the First World War. The boat concerned was *U 63*, and the deed was done by explosive charges on 29th October 1916, 135 miles west of Gibraltar.

MORPETH

Robert Stephenson and Co. Ltd., Newcastle-on-Tyne; 1902, 2,508gt, 310 feet

T. 3-cyl. by the North Eastern Marine Engineering Co. Ltd., Newcastle-on-Tyne.

The plain black funnel of *Morpeth* contrasts with the almost heraldic device on her houseflag, and sets a slight puzzle for the caption writer. The editions of *Lloyd's Book of Houseflags* for 1904 and 1910 maintain that her owners, the Morpeth Steamship Co. Ltd. managed by J.C. Adam, had a yellow funnel and a white houseflag with a red letter M. However, the same sources indicate that the Adam Steamship Co. Ltd. used a black funnel and had

a flag with the device shown in white on a red ground. Clearly, the Morpeth company was a venture of a member of the Adam family, and this photograph may have been taken early in the *Morpeth's* career when J.C. Adam was still associating himself with the family's main company. In support of this, and notwithstanding her distinctly ragged red

ensign, *Morpeth* looks quite new in the photograph. J.C. Adam's fleet numbered just four vessels; *Morpeth* being the first, with the last sold in 1915.

Morpeth herself was sold in 1906, her owners becoming the Dale Steamship Co. Ltd. managed by Lucas and Co. who, despite their Bristol domicile, had her re-registered in

Middlesbrough as *Milldale*. In 1911 she was sold to a member of the Embiricos family of Andros in Greece, becoming *Dimitrios*. Again, Greek ownership did not save her from German submarines, and on 6th October 1915 *U 33* captured *Dimitrios* and sank her with gunfire in the Mediterranean, about 240 miles north north west of Benghazi.

QUEENSLAND (above)

J. L. Thompson and Sons, Sunderland; 1890, 3,223gt, 326 feet

T. 3-cyl. by J. Dickinson, Sunderland.

Initial owner of *Queensland* is given as William Kish of Sunderland, a gentleman who only ever had two ships listed in his ownership, and was probably the designated managing owner for a group who owned 64th shares in *Queensland*. In 1898 this management function devolved on to Ralph M. Hudson, also of Sunderland, and whose origin as a shipowner dates back to the earliest steam tramps of the 1870s.

Queensland had the distinction of being the last ship Hudson owned, and in fact was his only vessel from 1915 through to 1928. She was then sold to F. Grauds of Riga who renamed her *Everita*. But even under the Latvian flag - notoriously cheap in the inter-war years - she seems to have been too old for profitable operation, and in November 1932 *Everita* arrived at Savona for demolition.

In the photograph, *Queensland* displays particularly good examples of two pieces of furniture which provoked considerable interest when an earlier set of Barnard photographs was presented in *Record*: the 'lighthouse' on the forecastle and the pole compass on the bridge. Note also the seaman high on the foremast, attempting to fix a broken halliard or aerial.

DALTONHALL (below)

Furness, Withy and Co. Ltd., West Hartlepool; 1899, 3,534gt, 338 feet

T. 3-cyl. by Sir Christopher Furness, Westgarth and Co. Ltd., Middlesbrough.

In the company of the other tramps in this feature, *Daltonhall* looks something of an aristocrat, with the white line on her hull and large areas of white. It is not surprising that the owners who had her built, the West Hartlepool Steam Navigation Co. Ltd. were involved in liner trades as well as tramping. In this shot, *Daltonhall* is in the ownership of Furness, Withy and Co. Ltd., also of West Hartlepool, who took her over within months of completion. This transaction, and her building at a Furness yard, was undoubtedly connected with the recent appointment of Sir Christopher Furness as chairman of the West Hartlepool Steam Navigation Co. Ltd.

Daltonhall was sold to Liverpool owners in 1914, and in 1917 became part of the Commonwealth Government Line of Steamers as *Australstream*. At the end of the war she returned to Europe to become the Belgian *Generale Degoute*, and in 1921 was sold to Greece as *Dimitrios N. Rallias*.

In her last days she returned to British, or perhaps it should be token British, ownership. The Scrap and Build Scheme was a worthy project to replace ageing ships and assist the shipbuilding industry, but a loophole allowed owners to buy superannuated tonnage from abroad and offer this in part credit for a new ship, rather than one of their own elderly ships. In 1936 *Dimitris N. Rallias* was bought for this purpose by Arthur Stott and Co. Ltd. of Newcastle-on-Tyne and almost immediately broken up by Clayton and Davie at Dunston-on-Tyne. This transaction, which also involved two other old ships, helped Stott to order the *Hopestar* (5,267/1936).